Eye on the World

Eye

on the World

GAVIN YOUNG

VIKING

*To Gritta, my 'Sea Anchor', for all
her dedicated help on all my books*

VIKING

Published by the Penguin Group
Penguin Books Ltd, 27 Wrights Lane, London w8 5TZ, England
Penguin Putnam Inc., 375 Hudson Street, New York, New York 10014, USA
Penguin Books Australia Ltd, Ringwood, Victoria, Australia
Penguin Books Canada Ltd, 10 Alcorn Avenue, Toronto, Ontario, Canada M4V 3B2
Penguin Books (NZ) Ltd, 182–190 Wairau Road, Auckland 10, New Zealand

Penguin Books Ltd, Registered Offices: Harmondsworth, Middlesex, England

First published 1998
10 9 8 7 6 5 4 3 2 1

Printed and bound in Singapore by Kyodo

A CIP catalogue record for this book is available from the British Library

ISBN 0–670–864919

The photographs on p. 137 are reproduced © Norman Sherry

If one writes about war, self respect demands that one shares the risk.
GRAHAM GREENE, *The Quiet American*

Introduction

I have written in another book that I fell into journalism as a drunken man falls into a pond.

But I was born a 'traveller' — and I hope to die travelling, just as my friend Graham Greene (himself a great traveller) liked to live 'on the frontier' or, as he sometimes, perhaps over-dramatically, said, 'on the dangerous edge'. Why I was born a traveller I have no idea. Unless it was that I was conceived at the Semiramis Hotel in Cairo after a ball in Kasr el Nil barracks (now the Hilton) where my father was stationed many years ago; it was a short step to the Semiramis Hotel from the barracks, as old hands — they would have to be *very* old hands by now — will tell you. Once or twice I managed to stay in the old Semiramis — the one I was conceived in, I mean — before it collapsed mysteriously one night when it was being 'rehabilitated'. I was lucky; because, of course, I couldn't stay there now; it doesn't exist. One of the first things I remember seeing was an incongruous ashtray on my nursery table with a sort of fork-like thing in the middle for matches and 'Semiramis Hotel, Cairo' inscribed in its rounded base. I wondered at the time why it was there — I was far too young to begin smoking (*that* bad habit started years later in the army) — and I couldn't understand why my mother's face flushed slightly — why she looked embarrassed — when I asked her. Now I know.

I don't think that was the only reason why I became a traveller. It was more likely something to do with the bookshelves in my grandmother's drawing room in Bude, Cornwall, lined as they were with complete volumes of the novels of Joseph Conrad and Kipling, blue and red covers with gold titles like *Lord Jim*, *Victory* or *Kim*, or the view from the upstairs window of the crescent of sea that I could see above the roofs of various houses (we lived on a slope), which made me wonder what lay over the horizon — cannibal islands? Cathay? Hispaniola? Any way, adventure.

I think it was a mixture of all those things, coupled with the fact that my father was a sailor *manqué* and I had an aunt, his younger sister, who

An idyllic snapshot of sunset in a Marsh village. The woman, or girl, in the right foreground has been spending the day in the reed beds cutting fodder for the buffaloes at home. The man is punting himself with a paddle — a common way of travelling casually through a village when it was calm and windless.

wrote and published stories and poems – in an impossibly old-fashioned style, but still, she did *publish*.

Whatever the reasons, I started travelling at an early age – if you think, as I think I did, that eighteen is early in a man's life. Iraq and the Marsh Arabs appealed immediately, and after that there was no holding me.

I only began to take photographs later on as a way of keeping notes. But I was not a professional photographer, even though some of the early pictures here appeared in *The Observer* newspaper. I always travelled on my own and often to unusual places – Nagaland, for example – so I snapped away. Because I had a good lens and knew enough to get the pictures more or less in focus, it helped the news editor fill space. But later on, when the unions – I suppose – said, 'Enough is enough,' and stopped me taking any pictures for the newspaper, I began to take them for my own interest only. When colour came into fashion – so much so that now it is actually quite difficult to buy a black-and-white film – I used pictures as an extra notebook – it is not always easy to remember what the colour of a man's shirt was two or three months later, or what a table looked like, or – indeed – *anything*.

Photographs helped one to remember. This was important to me because I wanted to put the reader in the picture, I tried to recall every last detail.

My first books had no photographs whatsoever; they were illustrated by a series of brilliant sketches by Salim. Salim, an Indian who had studied and then taught in England, was a fine artist and longed to accompany me on my travels. He was unable to do so because my publishers were never able to come up with the necessary and considerable sum of money, so he did the best he could – which was very good – from the text of the books alone.

Alas, Salim is no longer able to draw. He suffered a severe stroke at an early age, which prevented him from using his right hand – his drawing hand – and temporarily prevented him from talking. It is a fearful tragedy.

I hope not too many readers will be disappointed by some of these pictures of mine. I have done what I could to find the best of them, the ones that are in focus, at least. And I hope, too, I may be forgiven for adding in a text and captions, an explanation for what should be self-evident from the pictures themselves.

I am grateful to many people for help on this book: my editor Eleo

Gordon, my designer Helen Ewing, my copy-editor Sarah Coward, who pulled my text into shape, and, once again, my 'Sea Anchor' Gritta Weil, and Tony Mullins, who had been *The Observer*'s Art Director for over twenty years, and who was invaluable when we were gathering photographs and who knew which ones to choose. I also have to thank Khun Pitaya and his wife Dang, the owners of my favourite hotel, the River View Lodge in Chiang Mai in northern Thailand, for putting up with me for the months it took to complete this book, as they had put up with me in the past when I was writing *A Wavering Grace* about Vietnam. The River View Lodge is a simple hotel with a wonderful garden that runs down to the Ping River, one of the major rivers of northern Thailand. My friend Jon Swain also stayed here, on my recommendation, when he was writing *River of Time* against the clock. He loved it, too.

To all these people, and once again to the former editor of *The Observer*, David Astor, to Wilfred Thesiger (now Sir Wilfred Thesiger) and − now I come to think of it − to Ian Fleming, for having put me on the right track for my life of adventure travel, my most grateful thanks are well overdue.

1950s Early days and the Marshes

I had a vision when I was a boy. The vision was of the world as an apple. The point was that I was going to have to swallow this apple if I wanted to absorb the world; if I was to see every bit of it: every last desert valley and jungle path; every lane in Paris, London and New York City; every alleyway in Marrakesh, Cairo and Jerusalem. In brief, I wanted – I was *determined* – to see the whole world and digest it like food; like an apple, in fact.

I remember the feeling I had for that apple. It was just like acute hunger. I was ravenous. That is why when the first opportunity came my way for a bit of adventure I grabbed it with both hands. Another schoolboy, Tom Hutchinson, provided that chance. Tom was not a particularly close friend of mine; he was not even in the same house at Rugby, although we must have swapped dreams of derring-do at some time, I suppose. But his father had something to do with shipping and Tom lived with his parents in Hull, at that time a thriving port (before

This is me in the Tihama, the Red Sea coast of Saudi Arabia, in 1954 when I was with Desert Locust Control. I had come there after two years with the Marsh Arabs in Iraq.

the Seamen's Union succeeded in closing all the largest British ports, Liverpool, Manchester, Birkenhead and even Hull).

Tom knew of a ship that was calling at Fowey in Cornwall for a load of china clay, and he was to sail with it up the Channel to Antwerp and then return to Hull for more cargo. 'Would you like to come?' Tom asked. Would I be seasick? I didn't know if I would be seasick but I certainly would sail from Fowey, I told Tom. To hell with seasickness, I thought; we'll deal with that problem when we come to it.

I was almost eighteen and this was just what the doctor ordered, I thought, as I walked from the railway station at Fowey, a tiny Cornish port, late one misty night to find the vessel which was called, I remember now, the *Northgate*. It was January — one of the wildest Januarys for years. Our heels rang out on the deck when at last we found her, and someone called out sharply, 'Who's there?' It was the most unwelcoming first meeting with a new ship I have ever known: I had no idea then that ships could be so hostile. Only later did I learn that ships come alive only when they are at sea.

Next day, in the sunshine, we found that the captain was a genial Yorkshireman, and he and the crew took our presence on board as a bit of a joke. We had signed on as 'deckie learners' and we performed our duties, such as they were (polishing brasswork and sluicing away the china clay which clogged the decks), energetically enough.

I have said it was a wild January. The gales in the Channel that year exceeded all records and we had to ride one out at anchor in a fleet of ships similarly anchored off Dungeness on the Kentish coast. To my delight, the captain and his officers were all seasick. But, to my great relief, I was not. I didn't feel so much as a twinge, despite the rolling and dipping. The *Northgate* was too narrow for her length, and thus found it difficult to ride out those huge waves. I remember with pride when I offered the white-faced captain a Capstan cigarette and he managed to say, 'Thanks moochly, Gav.'

At Antwerp, although the city was in ruins after the bombing and shelling from the war that had just ended, we were allowed ashore escorted by Andie, a diminutive deckhand of about my age. By the bombed cathedral, Andie trotted confidently across to two tarts on a corner. He chose the taller of the two – she was at least a foot taller than himself. And afterwards he boasted, 'You've never seen anything like that before.' We had to admit we hadn't.

Later we went to a place called the 21 Bar that served beer quite cheaply and next day began the long winding sail to the mouth of the Scheldt, and then back to Hull. I was almost arrested in Hull. The police told me that I had had no right to sign on as a 'deckie learner' and go to sea when I was within a stone's throw of being called up for my national service. That national service (in the Welsh Guards), mostly spent in Palestine, started me off on my Arabian travels, eventually leading to the Marsh Arabs of Iraq, which in turn led to Arabia and journalism (I became the Middle East correspondent of *The Observer* after Kim Philby's disappearance in Beirut and subsequent defection) and a whole life of travel writing.

I wish all young people could have the luck that I had when I picked up a newspaper in 1952 – the time of Queen Elizabeth's coronation – in Basra, southern Iraq, and found the following article. It started something like this: '…When the moon has waxed and waned thrice, Wilfred Thesiger, the great Arabian explorer, will paddle his canoe down to the two long palm trees on the Tigris River and there under the Mesopotamian stars he will find two faithful Marsh Arab tribesmen . . .'

Some Marsh buildings were huge. Particularly the sheikhs' guesthouses (mudhifs); made of nothing but reeds forming giant columns which were bent over at the top and tied together. In these mudhifs travellers like ourselves would be able to relax and spread out as we wished. Perhaps the sheikh himself and his retainers would come to share coffee and a meal of rice, gravy and chicken with us. Sometimes baggage canoes (meshufs) would be dragged into the mudhifs and tied up there. The mudhifs were, in the strict sense of the word, guesthouses: you were expected to make yourself at home there.

and so it went on. Soon I discovered to my intense excitement that the two palm trees that the article talked about were situated only 60 miles north of where I sat in the British Club, devouring the damp newsprint by the west bank of the Shatt al Arab waterway in Basra, at the top of the Persian Gulf.

I finally met Thesiger at lunch at the British Consulate in Basra a little later that year and asked him to take me with him to the Marshes. 'All right,' he said. 'I'll be back for a bath in six weeks. If you can arrange to leave then, you can come with me for a few days.'

I needed no other invitation. I got leave, packed a bag – spare trousers and a shirt, cartridges, a shotgun – and set off. I did meet him near those palm trees, and very shortly I met and fell in love with the Marsh Arabs, their earthly paradise and adventurous life. Soon, too, I left the shipping company I worked for in Basra for ever. I was flattered when Thesiger

Hafadh. He is holding my Mannlicher .275 high-velocity sporting rifle, which I eventually gave him. Later, loading it, he got a cartridge jammed in the barrel and somehow fired the rifle. The result was he blew off half his right hand. He was lucky not to lose his life.

asked me to go back with him again. But I politely refused. I wanted to be on my own, and subsequently I went to the Marshes several times by myself.

I think the first Marsh boy who paddled for me was Hafadh, whose father – an old and grizzled farmer – I knew from Wilfred's introduction. Green swathes of rice, sugar and barley cut through the flat Mesopotamian landscape, interrupted by one or two men in long robes, men on horseback, and many birds. It was an idyllic setting. I travelled in a slender, long – 36 feet long I later discovered – incredibly sleek and beautiful white canoe. The boat – a war canoe belonging to a local friend, an important *sayyid* (or Shi'a holy man), Sayyid Sarwat – was propelled by four paddles wielded by four extremely powerful young Arabs the colour of butterscotch. They made the canoe – it was called a *tarada* – sigh through the water, rocking very slightly as it turned a corner in the reed waterway. These reeds were very high, sometimes 15 or 20 feet over our heads. Snow-white pelicans fished in the lagoons, storks arched overhead; there was always at least one eagle in the sky. Often the reeds trembled or crashed with hidden wildlife: otters, herons, purple gallinule or the huge and dangerous wild boar.

Ajram was another of my regular canoe men, along with Yasin and Hasan bin Manati. They all became good and trustworthy friends. On that first visit they sped the boat along at a dazzling pace with deft and powerful strokes. I saw other Marshmen in the prows of other canoes of the same immemorial design, bending against the curve of reed punt poles or poised to strike with their fishing-spears. Others seemed dressed for the warpath, clutching World War I Lee-Enfield rifles, with daggers in their belts and cartridges slung across their chests, they paddled strong and fast with a preoccupied air. The larger war canoes (the *taradas*, like mine) could carry twelve fully-armed men.

A chance newspaper cutting had thrown me into this natural paradise. Spiritually, I haven't cut adrift from it yet. This first early spell in the Marshes lasted about two years: the second started when I returned there in 1973 on a voyage of rediscovery after an absence of fifteen years.

Wilfred and I learned the language of the Marsh Arabs – a derivation of Iraqi Arabic. The only three Europeans to know the Marshes – Wilfred, Gavin Maxwell and I – all wrote books about their experiences there – *The Marsh Arabs, A Reed Shaken by the Wind* and *Return to the Marshes* – tributes, I suppose, to the fascination and beauty of the region and its people.

Canoe boys, with Hasan bin Manati (foreground, right). Opposite: Wilfred Thesiger in his canoe. Hafadh is in the prow on the left, the leading paddler, and Ajram is behind him.

We stayed in humble villages with no special food, no boiled water, not even insect repellent (the fleas and mosquitoes made the most of that), because Thesiger believed – and so do I now – that such artificial aids to comfort make breaking down barriers of race and upbringing that much harder.

Wilfred left the area for good long ago when the Hashemite monarchy was overthrown in the revolution of 1958; Gavin Maxwell, who was there in 1956 for a short period, died of cancer in 1969, aged fifty-five; and I persevered there until the 1990s when I was refused a visa to return.

My Marsh story ended in the ultimate tragedy. After showing an amazing loyalty and courage fighting for Saddam Hussein in the long eight-year war with Iran in the 1980s, the leader they had worshipped decided after the Gulf War to obliterate them and their environment – the waterways, the island houses, the water buffaloes, the birds, everything – for reasons of his own. The places where Hafadh and I and other Marsh Arabs had waited at sunset for flighting duck or geese – on still ponds that had been there literally since the time of the Flood – are now, I know, flat beds of mud and ruined houses without human or animal life of any kind. I myself am not allowed to return; the Iraqi government will not give me a visa. A paradise has been taken away from me

and the world. The Marsh Arabs no longer exist anywhere in the world; they are a thing of the past.

When I returned during the Iran–Iraq War of the 1980s – a war fought between two lots of Shi'a Muslims (at least, the Marsh Arabs were notionally Shi'a) – I found the Marsh Arabs geared up to protect the Marsh waterways against the Persians, whom they contemptuously called by the old, historic name 'Ajami'. The Marsh Arabs knew the Marshes were a stepping-stone to the oilfields further south and west.

Old Sayyid Sarwat, too, was 'anti-Ajami' and used to refer with scorn to the age-old defeat of the Persian army by the Muslim Arabs and their expulsion from the deserts of Arabia – although the defeat was at Qadisiyah in AD 635 and the Persian army of those days was equipped with elephants and commanded by General Rustam. Evidently, to the Sayyid as much as to the other Marsh Arabs, history and race were as important as religion. It was Sayyid Sarwat, after all, who on my return in the early 1980s again lent me his magnificent war canoe, which he had painted white so that we glimmered like ghosts along the reed-bound waterways and the lagoons of the Marshes.

He was the most revered of *sayyids*; tall and powerfully built, and embodying all that was finest in Iraq, in Arabs and in Islam. He was not in the least fanatical. On the contrary, he was warm-hearted and humorous and always reminded his supplicants that Allah was 'the Merciful One'. I often wondered if the Ayatollah Khomeini would have shown such unstinted friendship to a non-Muslim.

Sayyid Sarwat had suffered – willingly – in the war with Iran. He had lost two nephews in the fighting near Abadan and they were to be buried with him in the holy city of Nejef. For, to my infinite sorrow, the Sayyid himself died peacefully, aged eighty-six, in 1984. His youngest son Abbas, although he too was a *sayyid*, now wore the khaki uniform and pistol of an army lieutenant. He had been in action more than once and had been wounded quite badly in the knee. He had also been awarded two medals for bravery by Saddam Hussein – eight-pointed stars with crossed swords in gold on a black-and-red ribbon.

It was because of events like this – and people like Abbas – that a journalist had come to see me in Baghdad to ask if I knew that the Marsh Arabs were now national heroes. I was delighted. For years Iraqis from Baghdad had thought me slightly mad for spending so much time with Marsh Arabs, whom they despised as no-good vagabonds, illiterate at that. Now I was able to point out to the journalist that the Marsh Arabs were the inheritors of the pure-blooded Arabs of the Arabian desert whose virtues were thrift, hard work, courage, simplicity, generosity and reverence – virtues quite hard to find in cities like Baghdad. As for the Marsh women, I said, they had always been a back-parlour power in the region.

On my last visit to the Marshes a group of us, including my friend Sahain, punted out to a favourite lagoon to drink tea on a reed island. With us were Bani, Sahain's eldest son, who was resting between battles, and Khanjar, who had been in the war zone of Majnun, the scene of one of the bloodiest Iranian breakthroughs, where the bodies had lain thick on the ground. Bani, who pushed cigarette packets on to the reeds to serve as targets for our shooting matches with their Kalashnikovs, had been in fierce fighting east of Basra. We joked in the sun; heron flapped overhead; coot swam across the waterway – but these men, and others, would be returning to the front in a day or two.

It may seem strange today that these Marsh Arabs, soon to be so cruelly deprived of their water habitat and their age-old livelihood, were ready to save their country from the Iranians. Saddam is a Sunni Muslim, after all. But the point is that Saddam had once given the Marsh Arabs dignity, supplying them with electricity and piped water (before that they had had to make do with bilharzia-filled Marsh water); ice factories and government-subsidized motorboat transport to markets, which had greatly increased local income from fishing; as well as creating a demand from new factories for Marsh reeds to make paper. He had provided doctors and clinics in the Marshes, too. 'Soon the Government will pave the lagoons, and we'll all have cars,' someone joked. That is why Saddam, at that time, was so popular, and why 20-foot smiling cutouts of him stood everywhere with captions saying things like, 'Everyone loves the Supreme Leader.' It was a genuine cult of personality to match that of Iran's Khomeini.

That, I am sure, is one reason why there wasn't much local fuss over Saddam's draining of the Marshes after the Gulf War in 1991. Another reason was, I suppose, that the British had long ago wanted to drain parts of the Marshes (those parts of them nearest Iran, at any rate). In about 1918, a famous British hydrologist, Sir William Willcocks, had been consulted as to the feasibility or otherwise of draining a portion of the area and diverting the water into a third channel – or river – to match the Tigris and the Euphrates. This would have the effect, he said,

The Berbera, a net-fishing tribe. No Marshman would ever admit to being a net-fisherman; 'the Berbera fished with nets', the Arab said, contemptuously. Occasionally we came across Berbera fishing with nets in the lagoons, gathering their boats together in a circle, like wagons expecting an attack by Red Indians. To close in on the fish, I suppose.

of creating dry land on which sheep and horses could be raised, rather as the Beni Lam raised sheep and horses on dry land north of Amara. The idea was turned down then because, I imagine, the Marsh Arab sheikhs, who were powerful at that time in the government of Baghdad, disapproved; they had no wish to be reassigned to dry land. They were doing quite well out of rice, buffaloes and reeds.

Abbas said his father's funeral had been very grand. 'Two hundred thousand people came here to his wake,' he said. 'From Baghdad, Basra, Kuwait, even Bahrain. We killed dozens of sheep. And you know that my father sent for you when he knew he was dying?'

'Yes, Abbas. The message came too late.'

Near the stream that bordered the Sayyid's large house and his *mudhif*, workmen were building a shrine to him – a *marabout*. It would have a large tiled dome, said Abbas, and marble walls. But, as I have mentioned, the Sayyid himself would be laid to rest in a huge mausoleum in Nejef. 'All the local tribes came to my father's wake,' Abbas added, 'the Albu Mohammed, the Fartus, the Suaid . . .'

Of course, this was to have been a place of pilgrimage in the future. Though heaven knows what it is now that the waters have all gone. I have no way of returning to find out.

Because it was my first experience of adventure (and without war), my time with the Marsh Arabs was traumatic. It completely went to my head. I was with the Marsh Arabs, after all, on and off for nearly forty years, and during that time I wrote an article for the *National Geographic Magazine* of America, a book called *Return to the Marshes*, and made a film of the same name for the BBC with my friend Nik Wheeler, who took some fine photographs – much better than my old black-and-white ones. So it wasn't all wasted effort. Also, it was my *first* time in the wilds; and first times are always much more memorable than subsequent ones. I remember how London and my friends there appeared to me like minute insects under a magnifying lens. They had faded far away. Even my family – my mother and father – seemed distant. I felt I would never go home but would stay out here on the roof of the world; which, of course, in a way, I did.

Sheikh Abdel Wahed, our host on many expeditions to the Marshes, with his son.

Boats at rest by palm trees in a clearing on a calm and windless day. The canoe nearest the camera is a tarada. *The broad-headed nails can be plainly seen here, as can its steep, smooth prow.*

Saudi Arabia

A village market in Tihama. It is hot, probably near midday, and umbrellas are used as sunshades.

It was Wilfred Thesiger, of course, who suggested I should go to the deserts and mountains of south-west Saudi Arabia. We were sitting outside a Marsh Arab house at sunset, I remember, watching Marsh people swimming and spearing fish in the water around us.

'Arabia is very beautiful, you know,' Wilfred said. 'They wear a sort of kilt there. And carry a curved dagger in their belts. Their chests are usually bare and they wear fillets round their hair with a sprig of some sweet-smelling herb stuck in it. Very beautiful. You should go there. If you call on Professor Boris Uvarov at the Natural History Museum in London, he will help you get there. You would have to go, like I did, under the auspices of the Desert Locust Control people – they are part of the United Nations Food and Agricultural Organization [FAO] and their job is to go into the wilds – that would suit you, wouldn't it? – and kill off these enormous locust swarms in the deserts and mountains of Hijaz.'

So, naturally, I went – first of all to see Professor Uvarov in London, then to London airport to catch a flight to Jeddah, where the headquarters of Desert Locust Control was situated then. Shortly, I was on my

Two ashraf come to visit me in camp. Right: A well in the desert on the way to Najran, below Bisha.

way south in a Locust Control Land Rover, with a sack or two of poisonous bran to spread around for the locusts to eat. I also had a tent in a 15-cwt truck, and a crew — all that was needed for a long stay in the low plain that stretches from Jeddah to Gizan on the Red Sea. For I was going to the Tihama, the plain that borders the sea — not the place Wilfred had talked of so glowingly in the Marshes. That, I found out in a month or two, would come later. I didn't know it then, but my two years in Arabia would be divided into two periods: one, in the Tihama; and another — rather longer — down towards Najran and Khamis Mushait, the Asir province, in fact.

That was the place Wilfred had known — the place where people wore kilts and daggers and had fillets in their hair and lived in tall Alice-in-Wonderland houses.

Meanwhile I became accustomed to the Tihama, improved my Arabic (some of the purest Arabic was spoken in this part of Arabia, whereas the Marsh Arabs spoke a debased version of Iraqi Arabic) and found my way about the hills and wadis. I liked the people hereabouts. I soon met and made friends with a tribe of *ashraf* (supposedly distantly related to Prophet Mohammed, they were entitled by this fact to wear the square gold *agals* round their heads to keep their headcloths in place).

Two or three of these *ashraf* used to wander into camp and squat down and drink tea while I sat in my camp chair and inspected my map to see where the next 'kill' would take place — that is to say, where the next vast swarm of locusts would settle and spring on the lines of poisonous bran which we sprinkled from the back of the 15-cwt truck and which the locusts ate ravenously – eating each other in their eagerness to get at the stuff.

The local ashraf accompanied us on these 'killing expeditions' – partly because they were paid to help us but also, I think, because they loved driving fast across the plains.

I had a mixed crew: one man came from eastern Arabia, near Dharan, I think; another came from Medina, which was not far away in the north-easterly direction; and my servant was a gat-chewing Yemeni called Hasan, who continually badgered me to teach him to drive the Land Rover.

Finally, the time came to move inland to the Asir. Here, I thought, was the real Arabia. Wells in the desert, and camels, and water being hauled up in skins by boys with wild hair and ragged clothes. There were asses, too, in back alleys of small townships, and houses with solid mud walls.

There were grand houses as well; houses like fortresses, with huge doorways and gun slits; and sometimes congregations of large houses gathered round wells and palms and orchards. If you went into these houses you found yourself in small smooth-sided rooms with tiny windows with doors over them. The houses were tall and graceful. They reared up in the sky, and the lighted windows created an extraordinary fairyland effect at night. We liked to camp in an orchard and wait for the locals to visit us – which they did, at first shyly, feeling my clothes and the hair on my arms (they had never seen a European before), until at last their natural hospitality would get the better of them and they would ask me (all of us) to visit them at home.

A cluster of mud 'skyscrapers' near a well with palm trees in Asir.

1959 Tunisia

A bridge destroyed and a pylon hopelessly bent during the fierce fighting in the Algerian war between the French army and the Algerians, where I began my war-reporting career. A million and a half men died.

Tunisia was the country where – had I but known it – the *destruction* of war first impinged on my life. I should have learned a lesson.

At the end of my years in Saudi Arabia with Desert Locust Control, I went back briefly to the Marshes of Iraq where I met Gavin Maxwell, who had just spent three weeks there, finding his otter and arguing with Wilfred Thesiger. Gavin later became a friend of mine.

I then went home to England on leave. So it was there that I was overtaken by the news of the Anglo-French Suez campaign in cahoots with the Israelis, which left the Canal in Allied hands and the United States siding with Gamal Abdel Nasser against the Europeans. The monarchy in Iraq was overthrown some time later. The British and French were henceforth banned from the Middle East as spies and 'difficult people'. I found myself unable to return to Arabia and the locusts. Or, for the time being, to the Marshes.

In despair I took what little I could salvage from the Arab world – my knowledge of Marsh Arabic and of Islam, and my conviction that Nasser was right – and went off to the other half of the Muslim-Arab world; to North Africa, the Maghreb, where the French were engaged in a savage colonial war with the Algerians. There I got a job at Radio Morocco in Rabat, thanks to the presence of a rather wild but charming left-winger called Margaret Pope, who had become a personal friend of Allal al Fassi, the Moroccan opposition nationalist leader, and Moulay Ahmed Alaoui, later to become King Hassan's Minister of Information. Luckily, I could travel about Morocco – which is one of the world's most beautiful places – in order to design programmes for the English radio service about the hinterland of the country, from Tangier in the north to Zagora in the south.

It was in Tangier that I met a man who was to do a lot for me in the future. This was Ian Fleming; later to become famous as the author of the James Bond books, which made him a millionaire. His fame and fortune were in the future then; he was currently writing only his second or third book (eventually called *Diamonds are Forever)* and living at the plush Minza Hotel near the bar where I met him, Dean's Bar.

I can see the scene exactly even today. Seated in Dean's were David Herbert, Bob Lebus, Ali Forbes and Ian Fleming, a tall, good-looking man holding a long cigarette-holder in one hand and a pint tumbler of vodka and tonic in the other. David, a hysterically funny man, was – to use his own words – 'the Queen Mum' of Tangier, and lived on the New Mountain. Bob was just about to come to live in Tangier, encouraged by David, and the delightful Ali Forbes (although he may deny it now) was, as I recollect it, writing a 'Parliament Day by Day' column for one of the Tangier tabloids – before the days of telephones, telex or fax (I need hardly say). But it was Ian who was the important one for me. We got on like a house on fire. I told him about Wilfred Thesiger and the Marsh Arabs, and he called me 'his Zulu' for some reason, possibly because he considered the whole idea of my living in such a wild place really 'Zulu-like' in its bizarreness.

I must explain that Ian was not simply an author about to gain fame and fortune. He was already foreign manager of the conservative *Sunday Times*. When we met at Dean's Bar I was bemoaning my fate, complaining how I would soon have to go back to London to find conventional work in a nine-to-five job.

'Look here,' said Ian, 'there's only one job in the world that pays people to be independent, to travel anywhere on this globe, and to hobnob with heaven-knows-who from a president to a prostitute. That job is journalism.'

'Not a job for me,' I said, weak as dishwater. 'I can't write. Even if I could, my name appearing in print . . . too terrifying . . .'

'Well,' said Ian across his levelled cigarette-holder, 'you know where to find me.'

A year went by, during which I met and sympathized with Algerian intellectuals. I was not a born left-winger, but I saw that Nasser was riding on an unstoppable wave of Arab nationalism. I also saw that the Algerian government in exile (the GPRA) was based in Tunis and, even more important for me, that the British press was covering the increasingly bloody war from Paris and not from Tunis or Algiers. So, soon, I left my job at Radio Morocco and moved to Tunis. From there I took Ian's advice and applied to become a journalist. But I did not apply to join Ian's *Sunday Times*, which, being firmly conservative, had supported Sir Anthony Eden's Suez adventure. The letter I wrote went to David Astor at *The Observer*, which had taken a more (in my view) realistic attitude to Nasser and had lost half its circulation in doing so.

Tunisian peasants stand in front of their houses destroyed by the war.

I sent off the letter and was rewarded in due course by an answer: 'Would you please come to London and be interviewed by Robert Stephens, *The Observer*'s diplomatic correspondent?' I went like a shot, and was duly interviewed. Apparently my answers to Stephens's questions were not all that stupid, because I was shortly ushered into the presence of the editor himself. David Astor made me *The Observer*'s 'stringer' in Tunis, so now I was off and away.

Newly accredited as *The Observer*'s stringer I returned to Tunis and the war. Eventually the news editor Michael Davie cabled me for a first telegram for the paper. In a panic I typed it out and to my astonishment it appeared (much cut) in the next Sunday's edition. From that moment I was, I suppose, a war correspondent. I was to remain one for the next twenty years or so, until I began looking for ways in which to avoid seeing corpses, refugees and desolation wherever I looked; that is, until I found a way to find adventure writing books, and not on the battlefields of the world.

1960 Central Africa

Refugees at a mission in Burundi.

My first experience of warfare in Africa came to me in the ex-Belgian Congo. I was sent there – still as a stringer – by *The Observer* in 1960. Just after the Congo's independence, and after my efforts in Tunisia and Algeria, the Congo blew up into civil war. United Nations troops from Morocco, Tunisia, Ghana, Ethiopia, Egypt and other countries were sent out there under the eagle eye of one of the UN's toughest and brightest Secretary-Generals so far, Mr Dag Hammarskjöld. Patrice Lumumba lost little time in falling out with him. Lumumba had become the independent Congo's first Prime Minister but was killed mysteriously in a plane taking him to Elizabethville, the capital city of Katanga, the copper-rich mining state ruled at the time by his arch-enemy Moise Tshombe.

Meanwhile there were two other trouble spots in that part of Africa – Angola and Burundi (or Ruanda-Urundi, as it was called then – when it

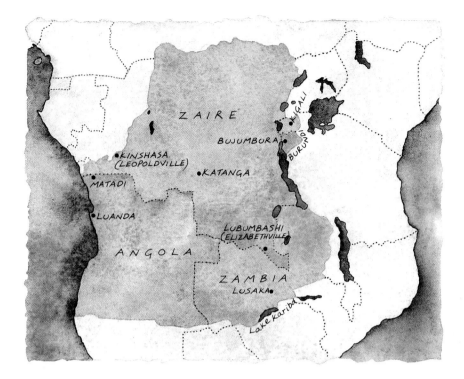

had been a Belgian colony, like the Congo itself). Dag Hammarskjöld was killed equally mysteriously, in a plane crash, while journalists and diplomats waited for his arrival at Ndola airport in what was then Northern Rhodesia and later became Zambia.

Roberto Holden was the leader of one Angolan group – called UPA – which had started the war of independence against Portuguese rule in Angola. He popped up in Leopoldville (Kinshasa, nowadays) at the height of the bigger Congolese drama, and he invited some journalists, including myself, to visit Angola and see something of the plight of the Portuguese army as it was being pursued by his rebels in the north of the country.

The Portuguese army may have been on the run but I didn't see it. Instead, when Horst Faas, a noted German war photographer in those days, and I and some other correspondents arrived in Angola, we found simply a number of deserted buildings and streams of refugees, but no defeated Portuguese troops. In the deserted village where we were staying I saw one Angolan soldier – possibly of Holden's UPA – who was armed with a Sten gun and wanted to pose with me by an abandoned jeep.

Horst got hold of some Angolan soldiers, armed with muzzle-loaders manufactured some time during the American Civil War. They wore headdresses shaped like helmets, I remember, but they were made from melon skins and offered their wearers no protection whatsoever. At any rate, Horst got them to pretend they were firing at low-flying aircraft. I directed them, and felt a little like Erich von Stroheim directing a famous film of the 1920s.

We walked around the seemingly totally deserted undulating plain, covered with wiry grass, for a day or two, and returned to the Congo the way we had come. We saw nothing of the war Holden had been waging – evidently with some success if the deserted villages and the jeep were anything to go by. His soldiers were a sorry lot, though, I thought, and although they were full of confidence in their future, it was difficult to agree with them that the Portuguese cohorts of Salazar were on their way out and that it was all for the best for the future state of Angola.

Nowadays I might feel differently about it all.

I first travelled to Burundi in the middle of the war in the ex-Belgian Congo shortly after its independence. It later became Zaire. The war there was one of the nastiest I have ever experienced. I soon got the vivid impression that all of us there would be consumed by the Congo (or, literally, by the Congolese, many of whom were cannibals) if we stayed there too long; by 'all of us' I mean diplomats, journalists, United Nations soldiers, civilians, everyone. It was a place where one moment you could be talking and laughing amicably with Congolese troops in full battle order, and the next you would have your legs cut off with *pangas* (machetes) below the knees – yet the only thing that would have changed would be that a sergeant or someone would have surreptitiously joined the group you were joking with and suddenly denounced you as a disguised Belgian paratrooper or a spy. Then the *pangas* would be applied to your legs with a vengeance.

Burundi was not much better. In fact, there, it may have been worse. The Tutsis were massacring the Hutus or the Hutus were massacring the Tutsis (I can't remember which) and this seemed to be a regular pattern of events every seven years or so, like the Years of the Locust. All I know is that the tall ones were the Tutsis and the smaller ones were the Hutus. I flew with two friends to Bujumbura and drove from there up to Kigali, then the capital of Ruanda-Urundi.

One of these friends was a young journalist called Dave Halberstam, later to achieve fame, or at least notoriety, in Vietnam; but then he was newly hatched from America for the *New York Times* and a former protégé, I think, of the famous Scottish-American journalist, James Reston.

Thousands of mothers and children were fed and housed in missions like this. Below: Catholic priests were often in charge of the missions.

The other friend was a British diplomat, who was the Consul-General in Bujumbura, James Murray (now Sir James Murray); a very bright and amusingly acerbic man who now lives with his wife in Brooklyn Heights, New York.

The pictures I took in Burundi were mostly situated in a Catholic mission that had been turned into a refugee camp or, at least, a refuge for the destitute. There were a good many of those poor people there, as later there were to be a lot more; it was a harrowing scene.

1961 The Nagas

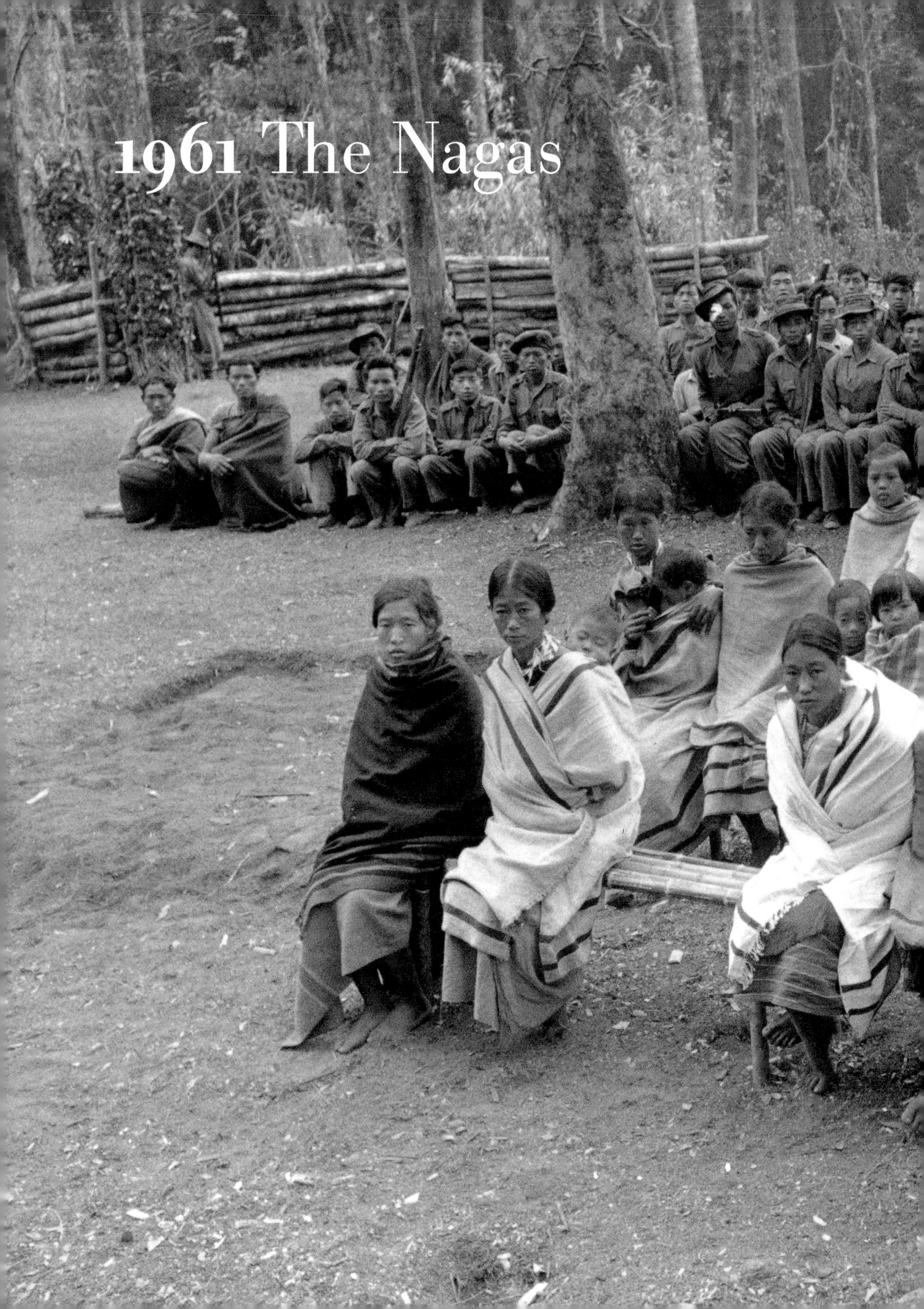

I suppose the Naga story began, at least for me, when David Astor sent me a letter in Africa which said, in effect: 'How do you feel about a trip to Nagaland? The war there looks like an *Observer* story. Come back to London and let's talk about it.' I was thrown into some confusion. Where on earth was Nagaland? I had no idea, but nothing would have induced me to confess to anyone that I had never heard of it. I cabled back: 'Agree Nagaland well worth a visit.'

The Naga story (for *The Observer* and Britain) began with the arrival in London via Switzerland of Mr A. Z. Phizo, who swiftly installed himself in an office in the Vauxhall Bridge Road and from some time in 1960 began propounding the Naga cause to the world, with the aid of David Astor and his friend Michael Scott, an Anglican priest with a courageous taste for odd, human causes. For years, 57-year-old Mr Phizo had been stating that case in vain to the Indian government of Pandit Nehru.

The Nagas are people of Mongolian extraction who are probably related most closely to the Dyaks of Borneo and certain Filipino hill tribes. They are stocky, muscular, cheerful people – a little like Gurkhas; at any rate, quite unlike the people of the plains to their west (the Indians). Nagaland comprises an area including the State of Manipur and the tangle of beautiful but savage jungle-covered mountains that form the eastern part of Assam. The Nagas are mostly hymn-singing Christians, converted by American Baptist missionaries who were expelled by the Indians soon after Indian independence in 1947.

The British had administered the Nagas on a very light rein. And Nagas volunteered for service with the British forces in both World Wars. Nagas served on the Western Front in the First World War, and when the Japanese troops were in control of the Naga Hill area in 1944 the Nagas remained inflexibly loyal to the British. Virtually the only exception was A. Z. Phizo himself, who later admitted he was won over by a Japanese promise to recognize Nagaland's independence. For the root of the Nagas's complaint was that the Indian government had not agreed to give them self-rule. The imminence of Indian independence in 1946 sparked off intense Naga political agitation for a

The Home Guards who came to welcome me on the border of Nagaland reminded me of – in fact, I took them at first for – Gurkhas. They carried .303 rifles, Sten and Tommy guns, and some of them wore daos, similar to the curved kukris (daggers) of the Gurkhas. Later, I learned that many of their uniforms and their arms had been stolen from the Indian army, or captured in raids.

44

separate homeland, led by the Naga National Council (NNC), formed
some years earlier to further its people's social and cultural advance-
ment. For the Nagas had once been headhunters; something the Indians
never liked the Nagas to forget. (To the high-born Indians, Nagas were
warrior-tribesmen dressed in bizarre kilts and carrying kukri-like *daos*,
which they used in battle to kill their opponents and then to secure their
trophies – that is, their heads.)

This degree of underdevelopment and the primitive state of the
Nagas themselves were used as arguments against Naga independence.
But the Nagas pointed to the independent status of the mountain king-
doms of Bhutan and Sikkim, and asked if these were not precedents.
They complained that the Indians chose to regard *them* only as semi-

naked savages. Then in 1960 Phizo produced a list of what he called 'Indian atrocities' against Naga civilians, naming Nagas who had been, he said, killed, tortured, raped and maimed by the Indian army. Rice stores and whole villages had been razed, he said. These allegations of Phizo's were forcefully denied by the Indian government, although the Indian press reported that guilt had been established in twenty-two cases of alleged atrocities. Phizo himself was accused of being implicated in the murder of one of his own supporters, and a warrant for his arrest was issued.

The Indian government then claimed that a compromise settlement of the independence issue acceptable to a majority of the Naga people could be reached. The now-accepted rebel 'hostiles', as they were officially called, were only 25 per cent of the population, the Indians said. Yet, nevertheless, some 30,000 (the figure was Indian, not official) Indian troops had been sent by the Indian High Command to suppress the Nagas who, according to Indian sources, were a mere 2,000 men serving in the Naga Home Guard, as the Nagas called their soldiers. The Home Guards by that time had been fighting the Indians for no less than six years running.

The only thing to do was to go there and see for oneself: first, whether there really was a Naga uprising; second, whether the Naga Home Guards really existed; and third, whether anything Mr Phizo had said bore any resemblance to reality.

I started out in a truly Buchanesque way – not by desire, I must add. My first approach to Nagaland and the east of India took me due north to the Scottish island of Mull. There, of all places, lived Mrs Ursula Betts, the greatest living non-Naga expert on Nagas in those days. As Ursula Graham Bower she had parachuted down to them in the war and been received, I'd always heard, like a white goddess. And from that remote island I went down to London again to meet Mr Phizo. Poor Phizo's looks were against him: he was small, like all Nagas, with long flowing hair, but the main thing I remember noticing about him was his face. It was badly contorted – whether by a stroke or something else I never discovered.

He was certainly worth listening to. There

I was escorted on the way up to Nagaland by Prem and two other Nagas. Prem (wearing glasses) met me in Rangoon at the zoo and guided me to the sampan that took us both to Homalin up the Chindwin River. Poor Prem was later killed in an ambush. Below: Another group of Home Guards, this time with a Bren gun.

I made friends on the way through Burma with a Kachin (one of another rebellious minority).

was no doubt that he was delighted to hear I was off to Nagaland. Quietly and imperturbably, over tea, Phizo said he would instruct his people there to send an emissary down the Chindwin River to Rangoon. He said I should wait for him on successive Mondays and Thursdays, in the Rangoon Zoo – he might be delayed by monsoon rains. Between the giraffe house and the monkey cage, he added without so much as a smile.

It was on my fifth visit to the zoo that I actually met the emissary: Prem – my first Naga. Fearless, impassive, resourceful Prem; a short, muscular man with high cheek-bones and a Burmese sarong. He had a tricky assignment, but he got me up to Nagaland and back again in two months, and in doing so became a friend. (Alas, he was killed a little later.) My progress up the Chindwin River took ten days and I had to share a sampan with Burmese policemen and soldiers, any one of whom might have arrested me and Prem at any moment. Under their inquisitive scrutiny I was obliged to impersonate a missionary. Prem was hidden in the very bowels of the sampan, which seemed to take for ever to travel from Mandalay to Homalin on the upper reaches of the Chindwin.

Once we arrived in Homalin, we had to walk over razor-sharp hills that were swept over most days by heavy monsoon rains; up and down, up and down, until the sweat poured in rivers off my body and I felt my legs would collapse under me. I was saved by the Naga guides who whenever I showed signs of flagging – which was frequently – took it in turns to push me from behind or feed me bamboo-shoots full of *zu* – the Naga rice wine which packed a considerable punch.

Lieutenant P. Vikura was the first Naga soldier I saw. He too was short, with extremely muscular legs, high cheek-bones and a humorous expression that is typically Naga. He wore the jungle-green uniform of a lieutenant in the Indian army and a bush hat turned up at the side. He carried a Sten gun on his shoulder and a Webley pistol and two hand-grenades in his belt. He might, I thought, have been a smart young officer in any army in the world. He was eighteen in 1956 when his father was bayoneted to death by Assamese riflemen of the Indian army. His

A view of part of Pagan, the City of Pagodas in southern Burma.

mother was jailed, and he had been with the Home Guards ever since.

Some of his men, I noticed, wore tribal blankets round their chests and shoulders, and several of them wore Gurkha kukris – the curved single-edged daggers – captured from the Indian regiments. Each man, besides, carried a .303 rifle and a bandolier of twenty rounds of ammunition; NCOs carried Sten or tommy guns. All were in full battle order and later I saw them kneeling in three ranks under the trees, heads bowed and hatless, as one of the sergeants said prayers.

The place we were aiming for was called Urra ('Our land' in Naga), which was a semi-permanent camp. It was one of four military base camps in the four Naga military zones, and housed about 250 Nagas: soldiers, civilians, scouts and refugees.

Neat, stoutly built bamboo structures faced on to a parade ground; the thick upper foliage of 60-foot trees screened it from the air; sturdy log stockades and a system of slit trenches protected it from ground attack. And the red, green and white flag of free Nagaland, with blue stars representing each one of its three provinces, flew from a flagstaff behind a

saluting base. The officers' mess was a long, spacious building with bamboo tables and benches under signs that said, 'Praise God from whom all blessings flow. Praise Him all creatures here below.'

All the Home Guards were volunteers; they were not paid, but fed and clothed. Expenses were met by voluntary subscription and donations. The main expenditure, naturally, was on arms, ammunition, clothing, medicine and stationery, which was used in large quantities by the Naga headquarters staff.

When I was there there was an increasing shortage of rice, normally the staple food. It was partly due, I was told, to Indian scorched-earth tactics; burning rice stores and so on. But a mixture of pulses, chillis, yams, salt, maize and a variety of jungle leaves cooked together in a massive earthenware pot made an excellent stew, I was to discover, and the four Indian prisoners held for a longish time by the Nagas told me they had become accustomed to the food now and found it nourishing.

A Naga People's Convention had accepted recent Indian proposals for a Naga State inside the Indian Union. Here the talk was of rejection and of Naga collaborators. 'We want to get rid of these Indians once and for all – they aren't the only people who can develop our country. Why shouldn't we invite technicians we choose and trust? You see, we simply can't trust the Indians any more.'

How many times in various parts of the world have I heard similar words about different masters – from Congo (Zaire) to Vietnam (Indochina)? Ho Chi Minh said more or less the same thing about the French years ago, and it took thirty or forty years of war to resolve *that* problem. I had only recently been in Tunisia, watching the Algerians teaching the same lesson to the French there.

The Indians have sometimes said that the Home Guards were obliged to terrorize the civilian Nagas into supporting the NNC and that the majority of the population was politically indifferent. The French and then the Americans said the same thing – until the North Vietnamese communists made them change their tune.

Image is still a major problem for Nagaland. Although Christianity has been a detribalizing and unifying force – every Home Guard recruit, if he is not already a Christian, is soon converted – the Nagas still feel bedevilled by their colourful past. Today there are many Nagas who are educated and bilingual – English is their second language – and they accuse the Indians, rightly or wrongly, of trying to preserve an image of Nagas as primitive tourist attractions.

A young Naga porter crouches by his house.

An Indian DC-3 shot down by the Nagas, who were well equipped with arms. The plane was flown by the pilot of the governor of Assam. I took tea with Naga officers sitting on one of the wings.

1964 The Kurds

A patrol of Kurdish national soldiers on a hillside in Iraqi Kurdistan.

Of all my wanderings, I suppose the Kurdish adventure of 1963–4 was the most exhausting. Nagaland, too, had been pretty hard to bear – I lost 20 lbs more or less, sliding and slithering up and down those jagged, rain-swept hills. There were no rains that I remember in Kurdistan, but the hills seemed very high and the rough tracks we took up and down them taxed me to the uttermost – perhaps it was the penalty I had to pay for two easy years in New York City.

At any rate, I arrived at the Kurdish border (or, rather, the border of Iran and Iraq in 1963) from Tehran, where I had been given a briefing on the Persian Kurds by General Pakravan, the scholarly head of Savak, the Shah's secret police organization (which was much feared at the time as being all-powerful and all-ruthless). In return for Pakravan's help I was to see the Shah later to report on 'his Kurds', as he called them. I needed Pakravan's help, as it turned out, to get from Tehran to the remote border crossing-point; he sent a car to my hotel and a chauffeur who knew the way and managed to avoid hitting anyone on the road.

Abdul Wahab, 'the finest smuggler in Kurdistan', according to him; the man who saw me safely across the border from Iran.

So my introduction to Kurdistan was heralded by a long, cold wait in a hushed valley, watching a protracted flashing of signal lights across the border, which seemed unromantically futile – or so I reported to *The Observer* shortly afterwards.

I was truly relieved and delighted by the final appearance of a mule-leading figure in a turban and baggy trousers who announced in cheerful Arabic, 'Welcome, sir. I come to take you to headquarters. My name is Abdul Wahab . . . Don't worry. I am the finest smuggler in Kurdistan.'

Clearly marked though they may have been on the map, Iraqi Kurdistan's frontiers on the ground were extremely hard to determine. The best authorities were the smugglers – like Abdul Wahab – who crossed them several times a week. The frontier region was a petrified sea of bare mountain ridges riven by deep, lush valleys and icy torrents. These valleys were often, in fact, wide strips of cultivation, fruit gardens and orchards heavy with grapes, pears and pomegranates, so the Kurdish peasants lived simply and well there. The hills that sheltered them sloped gradually from east to west until a sudden drop to the Kurdish cities on the plains – Irbil, Kirkuk, Khanaqin (the oil centre) and Sulaymaniyah, all of which were then held by Iraqi army garrisons that seldom ventured out except in massive convoys protected by tanks.

Motor roads were exceedingly few in those mountain areas. Armed Kurds thereabouts offered unfailing hospitality to friends and murderous reception to enemies; otherwise there were only stony hill tracks, usable only by mules, donkeys or on foot, that wound through village after village. It was formidable country and, unlike Nagaland, almost completely devoid of trees.

Because of this bleak landscape one was compelled to dive into caves (of which, fortunately, there were a number) at the approach of Iraqi Russian-built MiG jets nosing inquisitively overhead. When they appeared, or when one heard the jet roar booming back off high valley walls, turbaned goatherds and villagers peered upwards, shading their eyes against the sun. And on sheltered rooftops, Kurdish soldiers in battledress raised binoculars to inspect the aircraft.

'No bombs or rockets today,' a grizzled Kurdish colonel might smile. 'Perhaps they haven't many left.' Officers like this colonel had been in revolt against the government in Baghdad for two years. They were the leaders of an army variously estimated at 15,000 to 20,000 strong – the Kurdish National Army, it was called – under the direction of Mullah Mustapha Barzani. They opposed a far larger army and an air force composed mainly of Soviet jet fighters and bombers, but whose ranks had been seriously thinned by regular political purges. Iraq had been through purge after purge since the coup against Abdul Karim Kassem the previous year, and even some of the jets had been destroyed, too. The Kurdish officers were wondering how many Soviet-trained pilots were left and how many Soviet bombs remained in stock.

Myself wearing the Kurdish national black-and-white headdress.

The immediate aim of the Kurdish nationalists was a negotiated autonomous region for the million or more Kurds who lived in Iraq. Of course, other Kurds lived in Syria and the Soviet Union, and in the Shah's Iran. Eventually, they hoped, some realistic leader in Baghdad would acknowledge the impossibility of military victory in this oil-rich north-east of Iraq, and would be obliged to negotiate.

Typical of the 'new' Kurds I found was Jallal Talabani, then a thirty-ish, much-travelled intellectual who was also a dynamic military commander. He had led the Kurdish delegation to peace talks in Baghdad after the fall of Kassem, and some of his fellow delegates were still in jail there. Now he commanded two important military sectors and had become an influential member of the Kurdish Democratic Party's six-man politburo.

Talabani lived close to his troops in the field. A short, cheerful figure, he liked to sit cross-legged in a circle of partisans and villagers, explaining party policy, joking, dictating orders by the light of a pressure lamp, and commenting on news broadcasts from Baghdad, crisply and often acidly.

He told me then: 'It's not that we hate Arabs. I have an Arab colonel on my staff. We just want to be treated as equals in one Iraqi nation. We are not even demanding a separate state.'

Talabani and the then 49-year-old poet called Ibrahim Ahmed were the prominent Democratic Party theoreticians – Talabani described Ahmed as, 'Leftist, progressive, a bit like Sekou Touré [the then leftist President of Guinea].' Both men believed that one-party 'centralized democracy' was the correct political formula for an autonomous Kurdistan in a federal Iraq.

A young man wearing a similar headdress.

Talabani vehemently denied that the Democratic Party was communist-inspired, despite the twelve-year exile to the Soviet Union of Barzani, the then 59-year-old Mullah, the prestigious old man of Kurdish nationalism. Kurdish 'political guides' scattered throughout the countryside were at pains to explain that the communists were to be regarded as a threat to the nationalist movement. In one Kurdish jail I talked to several Kurdish communists arrested for trying to distribute communist literature. Talabani went on: 'Frankly, we would have been better off if the British had stayed [in Iraq]. Then all Africa and Asia would have rushed to support our struggle – it would be against a European power, you see, and thus respectable.' As for Barzani, he was no longer his people's sole inspiration and leader. 'Barzani is just one man in a national movement,' Talabani explained.

In the quiet, watered valleys, the bullet-scarred houses or the mountain caves many partisans lived in, the feeling of isolation was very strong for hundreds of Kurds who had given up careers, families and a whole way of life for this seemingly endless battle and hardship. Men such as Colonel Namek Abdullah, a middle-aged ex-regular officer in

Kurdish soldiers shaved every morning despite the harsh conditions of the war. They heated water in the kettle.

Iraqi prisoners in a Kurdish prison. Bottom: Kurdish soldiers cooking their own meals on the hillside. They survived mainly on rice, bread and chicken. The foreground is littered with chicken feathers.

the Iraqi army, with grey hair and a hard, lined face, who had said good-bye to a wife and four children in Baghdad the previous year and who now gravely explained: 'I talked the situation over with my wife. She insisted that the only honourable thing was to join the partisans. I've no regrets, even if my four-year-old son is grown up before I see him again.'

And there were men like one old, gnarled Kurd who had already lost two brothers and a son in the war. Clutching his Russian automatic rifle in a group of partisans forty years his junior he said savagely, 'Iraq has to get money from Kuwait and arms from Russia, Britain and America to fight us. They send tanks like flocks of goats up here. That shows how strong we are. I have given more than three of my family because every Kurd killed is my relative.'

It struck me as significant that more and more Kurdish recruits were young, city-bred and middle class. A high percentage seemed to be students, doctors and lawyers. Here, with Talabani, urban Kurds were fighting side by side with hill peasants.

The Kurdish way of battle was simple. 'We can't face the Iraqi tanks

Kurdish women sitting on the top of their house. One of them is knitting what appears to be a hat.

and planes in an open-pitched battle,' said Talabani. 'We haven't got heavy guns. So we allow the Iraqis to occupy certain villages, then isolate those villages, force them to call up reinforcements, then ambush the reinforcements. We're good at that.'

Because of tense tactics, and the consequent supply problem, Iraqi garrisons were few outside major towns. Often they consisted of 200 or 300 men in Beau Geste forts, unable to move outside. Inaccurate parachute drops of weapons had greatly benefited the partisans; they had replenished the Kurds' arms – which already seemed amazingly plentiful. Periodic Iraqi offensives had achieved temporary success, but decisive victory was frustrated by the impossibility of holding large areas of hill terrain indefinitely. On top of which Kurdistan was a land of milk and honey for the people who lived there, so there was no point in trying to isolate the Kurds from a city food supply and thereby starving them out. The partisans had plenty to go round. They ate flat bread, eggs, yoghurt and chicken stew from huge communal trays; sometimes there was lamb or turkey. They drank innumerable glasses of tea at all hours of day and night. Sugar and tea were smuggled over the Turkish or

Iranian borders, by people like Abdul Wahab, my first guide, or bought clandestinely from Kurdish or Arab merchants inside Iraq; so was the petrol for the numerous jeeps and Land Rovers the Kurds used – 'borrowed', some of them, from the UNICEF teams in Iraq.

Sulaymaniyah, one of the largest Kurdish cities, was almost completely surrounded by partisans, established on a horseshoe of enveloping hills. I saw Kurds manning camouflaged slit trenches with bazookas and machine-guns dominating a main road already blocked by tank traps and mines. Young Kurds described how they occasionally entered the city in civilian clothes and visited their families or made contact with the urban 'underground' groups, which reported on troop movements and the activities of Kurdish collaborators.

The time might come, said the Kurds, when the partisans would be strong enough to attack the larger Iraqi-held towns, like Sulaymaniyah. But, even if they took them, occupation would almost certainly be ruled out by the near certainty of Iraqi counter-bombing and swirling street battles in which Kurdish civilians would be the main victims.

And so the war went on. And still continues today.

A young, mischievous Kurd pretending to shoot the photographer (me).

1964 Yemen

A Yemeni tribesman surveys his homeland.

Mohammed Zubeiri, who seemed to be the only man capable of handling the negotiations between the Yemenis and the Egyptians. I wonder what happened to him.

I felt that in a way I was going home; I had been in these parts or very near them ten years before with Desert Locust Control. I thought I knew the region pretty well. After all, I had often pitched my camp just above the Yemen–Saudi border at Gizan. And I knew the other Yemeni border inland near Najran. So I felt no stranger to the hills and valleys of the rugged terrain that lies between Saada in Yemen and Khamis Mushait in Saudi Arabia, which was where the late Imam Ahmed's son Badr, the new Imam, had pitched *his* tents, the better to fight against the rebellious republicans backed by the dubious might of the Egyptian army of Gamal Abdel Nasser.

So I flew to Jeddah as I had so often done in the past for Desert Locust Control.

But things had changed with the overthrow of the royalists in Sana'a, the Yemeni capital. The old Imam had gone – he was dead – and the new one, Badr, as I have said, was in the hills of Saudi Arabia rallying the royalist tribes on his own behalf. In Jedda itself there was a sort of rear headquarters and publicity staff holed up in a hotel (which served alcohol-free beer, I remember) led by a strange American ex-seaman called Bruce Condé. This odd American had been in Beirut and had adopted the phoney title of Baron; so he was Baron Condé to the likes of me, whom

Yemeni soldiers. The one on the left looks like a young boy.

he treated with great contempt. Condé had ingratiated himself with the old Imam Ahmed and had been commissioned to design a set of stamps for him. Now Ahmed was gone and Condé had linked up with his son as a sort of public-relations guru. He spoke Arabic and behaved like an Arab, so he was not out of place altogether. He started by being very helpful to me, I must say, and led me to the Imam's camp by providing me with a messenger and a letter of introduction.

So far so good. But, of course, I had to go to the other side as well; to the capital, Sana'a. There I stayed with the United Nations military team – Canadians, I think – who took me in and fed me and generally looked after me very well. In Sana'a, at that time, were the Egyptian army headquarters and its commander, a General Moutagi. The Imam's royalists were supported not only by the tribesmen but also by the Saudis and the odd gaggle of British, including my old friend Wilfred Thesiger, whose heart, I am sure, was not really in the Imam's cause, although he hated Nasser.

The British radio station in Aden was the propaganda outlet for the royalist side. One day I heard on the radio that a place not far from where I was sitting in Sana'a had been captured from the Egyptians by the royalists with heavy Egyptian losses. I determined to go there at once and check on the truth of the report for myself. It is not often that such an opportunity arises in the life of a war correspondent. Accordingly, I approached the senior United Nations officer (a major, I think) and asked him to provide me with transport and a junior officer to check on the report. It wouldn't take long, I told him. Nor did it. We found the place easily; it was untaken; the position was wholly unchanged since a week before. No Egyptian casualties, no royalist victory, no republican casualties. The United Nations had guaranteed that the story was true. Naturally enough, my report (which appeared in the following week's *Observer*) infuriated the British in Aden.

Condé immediately sprang into action. He accused me to the United States and British Embassies in Jeddah of having been suborned by the Egyptians in Sana'a; and of having attended orgies in the headquarters of General Moutagi, a most respectable man, by the way, with drinks and girls and no doubt drugs as well. My friend the late Frank Steele was the MI6 station commander in Jeddah at that time and he came to me in some agitation. He wanted me to answer these allegations. So, having vowed never to talk to Condé again, I told Frank that I had been staying with the UN and that they would confirm everything. This they did, and there the whole thing ended. But I would never trust a 'friend-ly' face like Condé again. And it was lucky for me that Frank Steele was in Jedda just then. So Condé was refuted.

This is not to say that the Egyptian army did not take appalling casualties. It did. There were 25,000 to 30,000 of them there at one time, backed by tanks, heavy guns and jet bombers. Of course, the Yemen's terrain is very rugged, as I have said, and fissured with deep valleys between rocky escarpments. (There is also widespread cultivation that spreads in terraces, like fingerprints, round the hills – mostly of *gat*, the narcotic drug that grows like tea on the hillsides and which most Yemenis chew, pressing the leaves together into a kind of golf ball and jamming it into a corner of their cheeks. They then chew on it, gradu-ally absorbing the liquid of the leaves, until they become quite giggly – drunk almost.) So this war was a fluctuating affair of hand-to-hand bat-tles of arid defiles; of ambushes in which tribes stuffed their headcloths into the exhaust-pipes of Egyptian tanks and then hacked the helpless

When they weren't busy fighting, the Yemeni soldiers often passed the time dancing to drums.

crews to pieces among the rocks; of blanket bombing by the jets that screamed down on Yemenis crouching among the rocks of jagged hill-sides like hares hiding from hawks; of mines laid secretly in the paths of Egyptian vehicles.

Yemen's misery began in 1963 when a group of officers of Yemen's ramshackle army shelled the palace of the newly installed Imam Mohammed Al-Badr and forced him to seek refuge with loyal tribes in northern Yemen. The new republican regime, unable to stand against the furious tribesmen, called for Egyptian military assistance. By the beginning of 1964, 40,000 of President Gamal Abdel Nasser's troops were bogged down in the defence of his Yemeni protégés. In fact, this second near-criminal mistake by Nasser's close friend, the corrupt and incompetent Field Marshal Abdel Hakim Amer – the first was the hash he made of the union with Syria – turned out to be the beginning of the end for Nasser.

The capital of Yemen, Sana'a, which was the heart of this shaky republic, crouched on a tawny plain; a dusty town of narrow, tall houses built like forts, hole-in-the-wall shops, coffee houses and mosques.

By the time I got there in 1964 a UN 'disengagement plan' was in the offing by which the Saudis undertook to stop all aid to the royalists, and the Egyptians undertook to withdraw all their troops from Yemen. The idea was to leave things to the Yemenis themselves to sort out.

In Sana'a I met all the effective Yemeni republican leaders: self-styled Marshal Abdullah Sallal, the Neguib-like frontman of the republican 'revolution', and General Hassan Al-Umri, the nearest thing to a strongman in the republic. In khaki, decorated with crossed swords and Egyptian eagles, his answers to questions were uncompromising: the royalists, few in numbers, were powerless without Saudi Arabian financial and military support; if the Saudi government withdrew aid there would be peace. 'If the Saudis try to insist on the withdrawal of Egyptian troops from Yemen as a condition of settlement, they have no

chance of achieving any such thing.' What he said seemed to put paid to that UN settlement. Al-Umri also said that the hostile British in southern Arabia (Aden) must drop the royalists, too, and opt for recognition of the republic. This, I found, was typical of the unyielding position of the republican leaders; their refusal to co-operate with the royalists and their hand-in-glove relationship with the Egyptians who protected them. It was a sad demonstration of (Yemeni) wishful thinking and (Egyptian) lying.

General Moutagi, on the other hand, was a suave product of the staff college Nasser himself had passed out of. An invitation card arrived from him: 'The Commander of the Arab Armed Forces in Yemen.' There were film shows (no orgies) – a mediocre Egyptian feature film, colour documentaries of poverty in Yemen and what the Egyptians were doing about it.

The General himself was a short, broad, courteous man who spoke good English and studied yoga – he had just reached the 'self-control' stage. Another officer, with indifferent English, struggled to translate, and was occasionally prompted by the General. 'This is a defensive war,' Moutagi said. 'We occupy only the strategic points. The rebels are very good at ambushing. They are natural fighters.'

Behind the Egyptian shield, a desperate tussle went on to build a working administration. For centuries, Yemen had proudly spurned the paraphernalia of Western-style statehood. Former Imams ruled by decree based on whim. There was no civil service, no planning board, no budget, no bank. Yemen remained 90 per cent rural and tribal. The handful of Yemeni who had studied abroad had few bona fide qualifications for government. Thus, despite Yemeni shrewdness, the struggling civil service was virtually an Egyptian affair. In government corridors open doors revealed clusters of middle-aged men from Cairo wrestling with daunting mounds of paper. Egyptians taught in the few newly built schools. They tried to get Yemeni Airlines off the ground. Egyptian doctors worked in the country's inadequate hospitals and tried to modernize them. But, considering the state of Egypt's own finances and backwardness, such help was largely in vain.

Yemen now looked hopelessly deadlocked and embittered. It was clear that no solution could be found as long as the Egyptian army remained there. The disengagement plan put up by the United Nations failed because the forces involved seemed implacable, unwilling to lend an ear to reason. Sallal and the Imam seemed equally determined not to compromise.

73

There was only one man who seemed capable of handling the key to negotiations: Mohammed Zubeiri, a restless member of the republic's nine-man political bureau. Foreigners were not encouraged by the Egyptians to see him. 'What do you want to see him for?' I was asked by an Egyptian officer. 'He's not important here.' But he was immensely important. He represented a significant 'third force' in the Yemen conflict which seemed to be growing. I found him in his office one morning – a calm, dignified man with a neatly trimmed beard and traditional Yemen robes.

He believed that the Imam could return, with his family, as a private citizen to take his chance in future elections. He maintained that Yemen's future should not be influenced by *any* foreign power – which explained Egyptian objections to him. He was grateful for Egyptian help, he said, but would like to see Egyptian troops withdrawn – then there could be a 'Yemeni solution'. He pointed out that the withdrawal could take place when foreign support for the royalists ceased, and that Saudi Arabia and Britain, too, should end their support, direct or indirect. So spoke Mohammed Zubeiri, the leader of the 'third force' in Yemen. And in September 1964, the Yemeni 'third force' showed its strength. Representatives of most of Yemen's tribes gathered at Amran, north of Sana'a; some were royalist, some were not. The dissatisfaction of the tribes eluded government control. Zubeiri was elected chairman and the conference produced a number of resolutions, some of which were hushed up in Sana'a. Which means they must have been important, and anti-Egyptian.

Egyptian troops were alerted in Sana'a. Strenuous efforts were made to convince Zubeiri that he was 'tired' and needed a 'rest' in Cairo. But he was a brave man – he must have been because to engage in politics in San'a at that moment risked assassination at *someone's* hands. Undaunted, Zubeiri led a large demonstration in Sana'a in favour of implementing the Amran resolutions. He was a brave and loyal Yemeni, I thought – and still do.

It was since that time that I began to have doubts about politicians' good faith: their power seemed more important than anything to them. But other things matter to me. I think, in retrospect, that Yemen, Burundi and the Congo (Zaire) finally convinced me that compromise was better than the positive victory of one side. Vietnam and Cambodia were vital examples along the way. But the rot, so to speak, set in in the Yemen.

A Yemeni house on a rocky outcrop.

1964 Zambia and Zimbabwe

Young Zambian workers marching, full of enthusiasm, to their appointed duties.

It was fine and sunny in Zambia (formerly Northern Rhodesia) for Independence Day in October 1964. The Duke of Kent was there and General Sir Charles Harington, the British officer commanding in Aden (it was before the British withdrawal), and, of course, Kenneth Kaunda was the hero, the first black President of the old British possession.

It was all doomed to end in tears years later – but we didn't know that then. The expats were ecstatic – and half overcome by the oodles of booze that flowed so freely. People predicted that the fall of Southern Rhodesia (later to be called Zimbabwe) would be equally delightful.

In 1974 a general election was called in what was then still Southern Rhodesia. At the time I wrote a piece for *The Observer* entitled 'The Dream World of Ian Smith', a profile of a serious, rather po-faced man who was the last white Prime Minister of Southern Rhodesia, coming after such notable white leaders as Sir Roy Welensky and Sir Edgar Whitehead. The guerrillas of Robert Mugabe's Zimbabwe African National Union (ZANU) and Joshua Nkomo's Zimbabwe African People's Union (ZAPU) were already on the warpath to win majority

A morning constitutional in camp. Hair combing is important. (Note the 'Lumumba Flat' sign. That gives a key to the Zambian youth's political orientation at the time.)

Left: Some people were lucky. They were transported by truck. Right: Relaxing at a youth camp for workers, with guitars and a song.

rule. Britain had imposed sanctions against Southern Rhodesia's Unilateral Declaration of Independence (UDI) – these were only partly effective, and Ian Smith could still assure his Rhodesian Front audience (all whites, of course) that the Front would never hand over power to a black majority.

In 1974 I (and I was one of many) was declared *persona non grata* in Southern Rhodesia by Ian Smith. I wasn't worried. In a way it was an

honour, particularly as an official 42-page booklet of banned books included such luminaries of the literary world as J. P. Donleavy, Jules Feiffer, Mary McCarthy, Edna O'Brien and Norman Mailer. The whites of Southern Rhodesia were not great readers in any case – a few people may have read some of the naughtier bits of Norman Mailer, but that was about it. (I remember that the magazine *Playboy* was banned and that I had some difficulty getting Synge's *Playboy of the Western World* through the customs at Salisbury airport.) So I wasn't concerned about my sales going down – I was working for a newspaper anyway.

One had to say that Rhodesia was staggeringly beautiful. It was high up; even the plains seemed to touch the sky. It was the only place about which I could truly write – believing in what I had written – that 'the air is like champagne'. It was. And the countryside, full of flowering shrubs and huge, bushy trees and flowers of all sorts, was beautiful, too. I could see why Cecil Rhodes had fallen in love with the place all those years ago, and why the white settlers who succeeded him wanted to stay on.

Smith's Rhodesian Front won that 1974 election hands down. Just over 1 per cent of all Rhodesians voted for Smith, but as it was only whites who counted in elections he won easily.

Sir Roy Welensky, now dead, and Sir Arhn Palley, the courageous liberal who was defeated by only one vote in a partly Asian and partly coloured constituency, agreed that white Rhodesian ignorance was 'fantastic'. Government censors controlled everything – books, radio, TV and *The Rhodesian Herald.*

Racial mixing was minimal: whites ate and walked with whites; blacks with blacks. In sport, blacks played soccer; whites rugger. This *status quo* was as important in Rhodesia on the verge of independence as the white-dominated parliament.

Even so, Southern Rhodesia became the independent African state of Zimbabwe in 1980, with Robert Mugabe as its first Prime Minister. Unlike Kaunda, he is still there, as President since 1988 – and so is Mr Ian Smith, as a private citizen who decided to throw in his lot with the mixed-race community.

In the ruins of Zimbabwe in Southern Rhodesia. Old Africa had been virtually ignored until writer and anthropologist Basil Davidson drew attention to these ruins of an ancient African civilization. Opposite: I am lighting a cigarette leaning against an old tower in Zimbabwe's ruins.

1965 Vietnam

Quang Tri laid waste in 1972 by American bombers and North Vietnamese mortars. Note the South Vietnamese flags flying from makeshift poles in the ruins. I returned to this scene in 1996 to find little had changed (though the flags had disappeared, of course).

In happier times: Qué and myself in Hué in 1965. Right: Vietnamese peasants with boards denying any connection with the communists.

Most of what I have to say about Vietnam I have written in my book *A Wavering Grace*, the title of which is a quote from a poem by the English poet of the 1930s and 1940s, very well known in his time, called Herbert Read. The full line is: 'No might can win against this wandering wavering grace of humble men,' and I thought it suited the war in Vietnam to a T. The 'humble men' were the Vietnamese, of course; the 'might', in my time, was America.

The war in Vietnam was all about independence – the independence of Vietnam itself, of course: first of all from the French; later from the Americans. Both events culminated in disastrous defeats – of the French at Dien Bien Phu in 1954; and later of the Americans, who were evacuated from Saigon in 1975. There followed ten years of malice and economic penury under the new communist regime. The political atmosphere that prevailed during these years made it impossible for ordinary Vietnamese, who had not trusted either side in the dispute – neither the Americans and their

A South Vietnamese army 'hide'.

Saigon allies on the one hand, nor the communists on the other — to live there. They were forced to become refugees — Boat People — and leave their own country for exile in a strange, foreign land: ironically, the United States for many of them. Exile was their tragedy. And it was the ironic tragedy of many, many Vietnamese of the South, who had wanted no part in the conflict that was forced upon them.

Some of the worst episodes of the war, at least when I was involved, took place in operations with either American or South Vietnamese soldiers. The Australians were the best troops in Vietnam. They were all volunteers and had started their training in a jungle-warfare school in Johore Bahru in Malaysia, so they were the best trained in the country. In the end, the Australians were appallingly badly treated by their own government when they were withdrawn by Gough Whitlam towards the end of the war, and 'trashed' when they got home.

It was on an operation with an Australian battalion under a Colonel Broomfield that I first came to appreciate the Australian way in warfare. Broomfield refused all air support, even the American air force's offer of flares (the American flareships used to circle above all the battlefields at night; the American troops were thus reassured that the enemy was not

near by watching and waiting to pounce). The Australians did not share the same nervous tensions of the American GIs, which made the American conscript troops in the field so uneasy without those flareships overhead. The Australians were unfazed by the moving shadows of the bushes around them, and did not want the enemy to think they could be panicked into moves by such scare tactics.

I arrived in Saigon, sent by *The Observer* in 1965, just in time for the American invasion. Shortly afterwards I flew up to Hué, the old imperial capital of Annam in the centre of Vietnam, because I had been told that it was very ancient and very beautiful. It was both those things – and something more. The place was just about to witness the eruption of a Buddhist revolution – that is what it amounted to – and it was fortunate that I flew up there when I did, because I was able to meet the – 'my' – family who I still see even now, and who gave me a grandstand

I met a peasant family somewhere in the Mekong Delta. They might sympathize with the Viet Cong and worship Ho Chi Minh. But who knew?

Qué's father. He was illiterate. Mme Bong gave him and his wife free house space. He spent his days rolling cheap cigarettes for Vietnamese passers-by. Below: A Vietnamese family at work, making new bullets by sieving the soil from a battle-field. The words of Graham Greene come to one: 'We talk so glibly of the threat to the individual, but the anonymous peasant had never been treated like an individual before. Unless a priest, no one, except the Commissar, had approached him, had troubled to ask him questions, or spent time teaching him.'

view, so to speak, of those exciting events – and, what was even more important, from a sensible Vietnamese point of view.'

I met Vau on the plane – an Air Vietnam DC-6, I remember – and eventually Vau introduced me to Minh and Mme Bong, Minh's mother who turned out to be the key to my relationship with Minh's family. I still see Mme Bong to this day. She lives quietly in Saigon now, old and deaf. Minh is in exile in America with his wife and two sons. And so is Qué, Minh's friend, who also left Saigon to go into exile – sent there ironically and inadvertently by me a while ago, when it still seemed to him to be desirable to leave. It had taken a long time to get him out and by now it was really too late to change our plans, although Vietnam had become quite a reasonable place to live in once more, though impoverished. Qué was not spared the horrors of that long war: aerial bombardment by the Americans, napalm attacks, Mai Lai massacres, defoliation

*Above right: A Viet Cong
prisoner being interro-
gated by an American, a
South Vietnamese officer
and a South Vietnamese
'Special Forces' soldier.
Below: A South
Vietnamese paratrooper.
He asked me why I was
abandoning them. What
could I reply? He may
have died defending the
bridge between Saigon
and Bien Hoa during the
last days of the war.*

A South Vietnamese sentry surveys the ruins of Quang Tri. Right: An American officer at the prisoner exchange ceremony gives a cigar to a North Vietnamese officer, who looks as if he has no idea what to do with it.

and mass graves. But now all those things have ended for good. So have Hanoi's exclusive 'jobs for the communist boys' policy, the midnight arrests, the searching of houses at all hours, and the barking and bullying by communist cadres whose faces have been distorted into ugliness by years of anger and contempt.

My Vietnamese family had been lucky, I realize now. It should never be forgotten that the floor of the South China Sea is littered with as many corpses of Vietnamese refugees as ever made it into exile on dry land. That is a sobering thought.

But even so, Minh's family had to spend seven or more years in communist re-education camps and then face the fact that there were no jobs for them – they had not been with the Viet Cong, you see – and the fathers among them couldn't even afford to send their children to school. They had killed no one; they had committed no 'crimes'. Who can blame them for wanting to get out of it all; for bribing their way on to boats and vanishing out to sea, hoping that they would survive somehow and be washed up on some friendly beach?

When I arrived in 1965 the war was going very badly for the South Vietnamese army; it was losing a battalion a week in the Mekong Delta, as I remember it. This could not go on long, and the Americans were looking for an opportunity to land marines in Danang. This they did in 1965 and the marines stormed ashore (marines always 'storm ashore', if possible) into the arms of the massed international press corps gathered on the beach. The marines took some fearful casualties later outside Danang, and I couldn't help wondering whether the survivors of that

North Vietnamese ex-prisoners run through the river to be greeted by their compatriots.

North Vietnamese prisoners, stripped to their shorts, get ready to return to their side of the Demilitarized Zone. They are observed by North and South Vietnamese officers and one American (extreme right).

original 'storming ashore' felt they had been ill-served by the rosy feeling engendered by the cheerful smiles of the press corps that greeted them on that initial landing as they slogged through the light surf to establish their bridgehead on Danang's beach.

The Tet offensive came soon after that. I returned post-haste to Hué from America, from an interview with Mae West in Los Angeles as a matter of fact. I arrived to find that Mme Bong's house had been occupied by the Viet Cong and North Vietnamese troops for a month. The communists had also occupied the citadel and indeed the whole city, which the Americans subsequently blasted with bombs and shells and attacked with tanks in order to get the enemy out. As a result the city was seriously damaged; not as much as Quang Tri in 1972 which was utterly levelled, but quite badly enough.

But for me 1972 was the worst period in Hué. The North Vietnamese army had begun a sudden lightning advance down to the coastal plain towards Hué. Dong Ha and Quang Tri were destroyed and the South Vietnamese army units in that area put to flight. They poured back,

OBSERVER REVIEW

25 MAY 1975

...ace by the Perfume River for Madame Dinh (right), her granddaughter and two friends. Too often, like these peasants, they had to shelter from the violence of war as Vietcong, North Vietnamese and Americans fought over their country.

A FAMILY AT WAR

The Observer Review *Front of the fall of Saigon and my story of Mme Bong's family.*

Mme Bong (extreme right in both pictures) in a field during ceasefire year, 1973; and with her friends by the lake at Hué.

down the Street Without Joy, as the French had named it, throwing away their weapons and their uniforms as they went. I had never before seen such a rout in my life. It made it very difficult for me to escape from the front line (wherever that was) to Hué. And in Hué I found the Bong house empty and the South Vietnamese soldiers, who had fled and reached Hué, setting the market on fire and cavorting drunkenly beside the flames, still throwing off their uniforms. Terrified, I was certain that if I stayed there I should become their next target. I crossed the bridge and sought refuge in the modern hotel opposite the blazing market. That night was the worst I have ever spent. I was convinced – and I think every Vietnamese I met was too – that the communists would enter the city that night. I would have been murdered in my bed if they had.

The next year there was a ceasefire. I returned once more to Hué. This time I found Madame Bong and her family still there, and we enjoyed the calm and the absence of gunfire in the hills. I went with Madame Bong to the grave of her son and my friend, Van, killed in 1967 and buried in Hué in the family graveyard in Nui Binh. Then we wandered among the lakes and water tanks of the royal tombs and the countryside around Hué. This, I remember thinking, is the *real* Vietnam at last. All the rest: the bodies, the routs, the blazing markets, the ideological talk from North to South, is gobbledegook; not Vietnam at all. Vietnam is *here*, I thought, and still think. I have Madame Bong to thank for appreciating that, and it is a big 'thank you'. But Madame Bong is old and deaf in Saigon now; far from those tombs and that countryside.

94

In 1973 it was not long before a mass transfer of prisoners was arranged to take place on the banks of the river that separated Quang Tri from the northern side. The prisoners were all from the North, as far as I could see; none from the South at all. They had been well looked after. They were beefy men, dressed only in shorts because they had contemptuously discarded the clothes the Southerners had given them. Among them were North Vietnamese officers, some in solar topees. The North Vietnamese laid it on as a good propaganda exercise. There were some South Vietnamese officers and Americans as well — but the focus was evidently on the mass transfer ceremony. Speeches were made in various languages, American officers offered North Vietnamese huge cigars which the North Vietnamese accepted, smiling. What they did with them afterwards I never knew; the cigars looked too big for them to handle. And then the prisoners ran into the waters of the river and waded towards the northern bank to their freedom. They were ecstatically welcomed by their fellow communists and led cheering to the far shore. It was a great communist propaganda victory. It matched the US marines' 'storming ashore' episode of 1965 at Danang. It had looked then as if the war would soon be over — who could resist the American marines? But now here we were, eight years later, and within two years of an American and South Vietnamese defeat of shattering proportions.

It was appropriate in a way that the transfer took place against the backdrop of the ruins of Quang Tri — and the North and South Vietnamese officers and Americans were all present. I pointed out the ruins to various North Vietnamese officers, asking them if it was necessary to ruin a town in order to win a war. Needless to say, I got no worthwhile answers.

I went back to Quang Tri after the war — *long* after the war, in 1996 — and found the place still in ruins. The only thing that had changed was that the South Vietnamese flags were no longer there, and some little makeshift stalls and ramshackle coffee shops had sprung up on the edge of the main street. There seemed to be only one street left, and I and my driver, Mr Ha, sat disconsolately at a table drinking coffee, surrounded by what looked very like the ruins of a dead town.

Perhaps it wasn't dead really, but it certainly seemed like it to me. It was eery; since its destruction twenty-four years earlier little had been done to rebuild the place. It was still a casualty of war — and that is how I shall remember it.

In fact, it looked like a smaller version of Vietnam itself; a microcosm

Mme Bong kneels to light joss-sticks at the tomb of her son Van, killed in action in 1967. The tomb is at Nui Binh in Hué.

of a country that had been ravaged by war and had only barely survived. A place that twenty-three years after the fighting had ended was still struggling to make ends meet – poor, but independent and free at last; a pathetic relic of things that had once been better and a reminder that they would be better again, in time – how much time no one could tell.

Whenever I think of Vietnam – the war, I mean – I think of Hué during the Tet holiday of 1968, and of Quang Tri, destroyed in the North Vietnamese invasion of 1972 by the North and the South and the Americans. And of my return to it in 1996 with Mr Ha, and our miserable coffee in the main street of the ruined town.

But there is another more hopeful side to Vietnam. The aftermath of our coffee, as I relate in *A Wavering Grace*, was that Mr Ha and I drove back to Hué and I bought him some eyeglasses. Ha then said to me, 'You know something, Pappa? If this car was mine I would drive you all over Vietnam for nothing.' And I felt a surge of affection for Vietnamese who would say something like this and obviously mean it. He soon added, 'You must come to my home. Come to dinner. Tomorrow?'

I went, of course.

1970 Cambodia

I went to Cambodia in 1970 and was lucky to leave it at all. Of all the wars I reported, I think Vietnam and Cambodia were the most dangerous. With Cambodia leading by a short head.

For one thing, in Cambodia there was no official transport for journalists as there was in Vietnam where one was regularly ferried about by American helicopters – or could be evacuated from a tight spot in a countryside riddled with merciless communist troops. In that respect we were spoiled in Vietnam.

In Cambodia, when a journalist went outside Phnom Penh he was

A market in Phnom Penh. Most Cambodians rode bicycles or motorbikes since cars were very expensive. Below: A scene on the Mekong River at Phnom Penh.

on his own in his car and he was only safe again when he got back. No other foreigners ventured out, certainly no businessmen, and diplomats were not allowed to. More than twenty correspondents were reported missing in the six months after March 1970. The most recent, Frank Frosch of United Press International, a quiet, amiable man with whom I had discussed these risks in August, was beaten and shot to death 20 miles from Phnom Penh in November.

Of course, Cambodia could be very beautiful. It had gurgling rivers and green jungle trees, and huge flowers of wondrous colours with trumpet-shaped, pendulous mouths that glowed and glimmered at you from the roadsides. In Phnom Penh itself there were markets in which

A pagoda in Cambodia. They tend to resemble Thai temples.

everything seemed to be sold – everything from bicycles to cigarettes. There was even a brothel (which I admit I didn't see) where a sign said: 'Cunilingus spoken here' (although that was a story put out by Donald Wise, the much-experienced *Daily Express* man, who was also a wit).

There were also temples that glistened with gold like those in Thailand and glamorous old French colonial buildings in avenues of flowering trees. Phnom Penh was small, and, to me, it was an attractive place of temples and packed streets lined with cafés, restaurants and simple hotels, and one rather grand one where people paid enormous sums to swim and drink long drinks made of vodka and fruit juice.

Of course, towards the end – when the Khmer Rouge was closing in – it became less of a joke. It became, in fact, positively dangerous: the Khmer Rouge rockets were slamming into the capital fairly regularly. Each one demolished someone or something.

The odd thing was that no one knew, or seemed to care, what the Khmer Rouge would do when – or if – they entered the city. Certainly no one could have dreamt of the hideous massacres that would do for more than a million Khmers very shortly. I remember Ieng Sary, the murder-

A ruined old French house in the countryside outside Phnom Penh.

ous Pol Pot's so-called foreign minister, in Bangkok at the Oriental Hotel after the Khmer Rouge victory, giving a lecture with slides on the beauties of Pol Pot's Khmer Rouge regime. I took great pleasure in *not* shaking his hand at the end of it – though many other journalists did.

One British television camera team I remember very well. I met them in a small town not far from the capital. Their camera was loaded on to a bullock cart and the whole team belonged to Thames TV, although I am not sure. At any rate, they seemed to demonstrate the singular courage and initiative of journalists of all nationalities at that time. I never saw what they filmed, or in fact any of their programmes at all; I was too busy where I was – in Cambodia and Vietnam alternately. Nor can I recall any of their names. All I know is that they deserved to win awards of some sort for enterprise and derring-do in extremely exasperating circumstances.

Apropos the Great Cambodian Death (as I call the 'Killing Fields') there is a story I should like to retell – a true story. On my shelf as I write this are two tiny dancing dolls. They are in Cambodian dress. And this is the story: soon after my arrival in Phnom Penh I met two students, a brother and his sister; I can't remember their names; but they soon became my friends. Their middle-aged father was a junior official at the Ministry of Education, I think.

Shortly before the fall of Phnom Penh I returned to Cambodia from Vietnam and met the brother and sister at a dance they had invited me to. Aware, as we all were by then, of some impending danger, I pleaded with them to leave the country. 'You should get out at once,' I said. 'Go to Bangkok. Just for a holiday. See how things turn out.'

They refused. They told me they had exams next month. Very important exams, they said. It was the last time I saw them.

To this day I don't know — and I never will now — whether the sister had doubts. At any rate, she said as we parted, 'Please excuse. These are for souvenirs. Until you come back.' She handed me a small bamboo box; inside lay the two dolls. Later I had a letter from her; I opened it in Paris. It sounded fairly desperate: 'Things are not normal,' she wrote, uncertainly, 'less calm. Oh, how hard it is.'

Pol Pot's rockets were beginning to fall ever more heavily on the capital. There would be no exams that year or even the next. I wrote immediately, saying, 'Run — run — for the Thai border. Leave the country! I implore you! Don't waste a second. Exams are dead! *Save yourselves!*' I underlined the last words several times.

Phnom Penh fell to the Khmer Rouge shortly afterwards. A few months later Pol Pot and his colleagues, who had planned the whole affair over coffee in a Paris café, began purging the population of the cities, towns and villages of Cambodia. The people were driven into the countryside — the sick, the old, the dying; no exceptions. The hospitals and universities were emptied and their occupants tortured to death or otherwise killed — all in the service of the regeneration of Cambodian Man.

I never heard another word from my friends. Yet, as I write this — in 1997 — Thai papers say that Pol Pot is sick and dying, and about to be betrayed by his colleagues, Khien Samphan and Ieng Sary. Nobody knows what to make of this story. The truth is elusive, as usual. The Thais are hopelessly confused. So is King Sihanouk of Cambodia in Beijing. (The Chinese were the only country in the world to support Pol Pot's Khmer Rouge: that should never be forgotten.)

All that is left for me of that hideous experience are the two tiny dancing dolls, the souvenirs of two innocent and beautiful children, who no doubt were killed by starvation or, perhaps, by machete blows, for disobeying the orders of a madman.

The intrepid Thames TV crew from Britain who, in the absence of other transport, hired a bullock cart to take them around the countryside. Here they pass a ruined, though modern, French house, which had been hit by a mortar round by the look of it. Below left: The TV crew preparing to shoot a scene somewhere. And (right) a mortar crew preparing to shoot at a target somewhere.

1975 Iran

His former Imperial Majesty Mohammed Reza Pahlavi, Shah of Shahs, Light of the Aryans, was a complex man who could be likeable. Many young Persians called him 'tyrannous' and even 'murderous' – they were supporters mostly of the exiled and aged Ayatollah Khomeini, the Shah's sworn enemy, who was living in the neighbourhood of Paris.

The Shah sometimes appeared gentle and even humorous. What a nice man, you thought, emerging from an audience. Yet his secret police organization, Savak, was among the largest and most oppressive in the world. Khomeini finally deposed the Shah, who eventually died of cancer in Egypt. Since then Iranians have learned to live in another sort of dictatorship – that of the Muslim mullahs of Iran whom Khomeini put in positions of power before *he* died.

The Shah's great mistake, in my view, was to hark back continually to the pre-Islamic glories of Ancient Persia – the Persia of the kings: Cyrus, Darius and Xerxes; the Persia of the ancient city of Persepolis. Anyone could see that the country was not Ancient Persia but almost wholly Muslim, and that the Shah's most dangerous enemies were Muslim clergymen, like Khomeini, from the Holy Muslim city of Qom.

The Shah might have survived if he hadn't relied so obviously on America (the 'Great Satan' according to Khomeini) and if he had ever once bothered to deny that Savak used torture and other strong-arm methods (including murder) to make its presence felt. He could have put a stop to this. But he didn't; only saying, in effect, 'Every country uses torture. Show me the country that doesn't.'

But it was well known that several thousands of students and other opponents had suffered 'very bad' to 'shocking' treatment in the Shah's – and Savak's – jails, even if the bear pits, which Savak had once made use of, were no more. People, including lawyers, were kept for months

Triumphal arches at Persepolis. One such leads to another. It was here that the Shah held his vast state banquet in 1971.

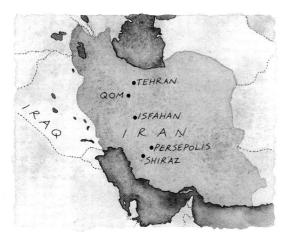

without access to family or the legal system. It could hardly have come as a surprise in this volatile political climate when the Iranian Brigadier-General, Zandipur of Savak, was killed on the way to work and two American colonels were shot dead outside Tehran. Muslim clerics fought with appalling mob violence against rights for women, land reform and the growing American presence they saw as threatening Muslim Iran.

Yet the Shah did nothing about it. 'Islamic Marxism' was the name the Shah's opponents gave to themselves, and they were very active, despite Savak's wide-ranging powers. Before the great state banquet the Shah gave to visiting Heads of State at Persepolis in 1971 there was a wave of arrests. A pleasant foretaste of the dinner to come.

But both Persepolis and Isfahan are jewels. Persepolis is a palace of an enormous escarpment and caves – each one the tomb of an ancient Persian king. Rows of noble arches in stone, with bas-relief figures on huge, heavy columns, follow one after the other in man-made symmetry. The tombs of Darius, Artaxerxes and Xerxes are here, carved out of the living rock of the escarpment above Shiraz. The tomb of Cyrus the Great is here, too. You can see why the Shah was so particular to identify himself with the Persian past. It *was* glorious, even if it was also brutal and bloody.

Isfahan is a different kettle of fish. It is a place of pigeon-lofts and religious Islamic schools (*medresas*), arches and mosques; a place where bridges spread themselves over the landscape and span gentle rivers that look like the rivers you see on old Persian paintings. Some of the older pigeon-lofts have crumbled by now, but this does not detract from them; they are still picturesque and still continue to attract birds, who flock to them. Isfahan has quite a different feel to Shiraz, where tourists gathered and the British and Americans used to try out their tanks before presenting them to the Shah, who was doing his best to turn old Iran into modern Japan. Against the odds as it turned out. There was something of Ozymandias about him I always thought: 'Look on my works, ye mighty, and despair.'

I have thought that if the Shah had behaved more like the King of Thailand he might have lasted longer on the throne of his country. With hindsight it was his eagerness to emulate Japan that was his undoing.

There were one or two grave endemic disabilities in Iran under the

Isfahan: the courtyard of a medresa, *a religious school.*

The inside of a ruined
pigeon-loft. There are
many of them scattered
about the countryside
around Shiraz and
Isfahan. Some are still
used by the birds.

Shah. For one thing there was Iran's inadequate labour supply: there was simply no workforce capable of building an industrial estate. A lack of foremen, supervisors, bank clerks, trained civil servants and electronics experts slowed projects down by creating bottlenecks, just as bad roads trapped mountains of supplies at too few ports.

Towards the end of his reign you met foreign workers everywhere – mainly Koreans, Filipinos, Pakistanis, British and French. And, of course, Americans . . . There were even, in the end, a hundred American pilots teaching Iranians to fly Bell helicopters at Isfahan; they once revolted against sanitary and safety standards, and you couldn't blame them. But once more an ancient people and culture were being assailed by a strident American presence – poised to amount to about 50,000, with wives and kids, large cars and money to burn. In beautiful Shiraz – the 'nest of singing birds' of the poets Sa'adi and Hafez – music, rose gardens and nightingales would have to struggle to survive alongside a new electronics centre and polluted water. Would the domes of Isfahan disappear in the clamour of seventeen industrial satellite towns being built round it? I waited and wondered.

A typical representation of an ancient Persian King (I forget which one) with a servant carrying a sunshade to protect him from the scorching heat.

A good view of the ruins of Persepolis.

1970s Slow Boats

I have said somewhere that one can only cover wars for so long without becoming sickened by the whole business of death, destruction and refugees. For me that had begun with the fighting in Tunisia, and had got gradually worse, culminating in the wars in Cambodia and Vietnam. Tunisia, as I said – and the whole Algerian War, where a million and a half died – was full of violence, the French bombing and shelling bridges, railway lines, pylons and so on, from Sakiet Sidi Youcef to Bizerte. Cambodia was bad, too – full of French colonial houses shattered by shellfire and bombs. As for Vietnam . . .

So it was with great relief in the late 1970s that I finally plucked up enough courage to cut adrift from journalism – more or less – and strike out on my own. It was a risk, I knew that; but one that I thought had to be taken. But where to go? And what to do?

As it happened, I had recently read a book called *The Great Railway Bazaar* by a writer I'd never heard of called Paul Theroux. I was impressed. Here, I thought, was a format that would suit me; a long series of lonely travels, and a book at the end of it. I liked trains – but I thought ships much more exciting. I believed then, as I still do, that ships were more interesting in themselves than trains – more varied for one thing – and ports more interesting than railway stations, or airports for that matter. Then there was the variety of crews.

When I put this idea to my new agent, Gillon Aitken, he agreed with me. Furthermore, he promptly found a publisher who was prepared to pay me what I then considered a princely sum to go from Europe to China by boat; cargo boats I had stipulated, and he had agreed enthusiastically.

So off I went. The actual steps I took that led up to my embarkation on the motor vessel *Alcheon* at Piraeus – the first of the forty ships that were to take me from Greece and back to Plymouth – are set out in the

The Cecil Hotel, Alexandria, was an old one, a throwback to the days of my father's youth. (I was conceived in the larger, but similarly old, Semiramis Hotel in Cairo.) It was in fine condition, too, with a buggy and its driver and a Nubian boy in a jellaba and (usually) red tarboosh who operated the lift, which looked like a black birdcage and moved very, very slowly. I loved the Cecil, almost as much as I loved the equally old Trianon Bar with its Italian murals.

Prelude to my book *Slow Boats to China*. This book sets out in some detail what happened to me on the twenty-three vessels that took me to Canton and Hong Kong. I had intended to write a sort of literary *pot au feu*, a mixture of what happened in this voyage and other things that had happened to me in my years as a war correspondent. When I arrived in Hong Kong various journalists whom I had known in the Congo or elsewhere – Donald Wise, Richard Hughes, Marsh Clark – were there to greet me, so they came into the book as well. It is nice to see old friends again – even in one's own books. I hope readers of my 'ship' books will be amused to meet them, too.

The writing of the book was done in Asia; at Raffles Hotel, Singapore. This was the old Raffles – before it was tarted up into the expensive place it is now. It was run by a charming Italian from Trieste called Roberto Pregarz, and the book took several months to write in a room at the back with a table overlooking the garden where mynah birds stalked and squawked. Then I took what I'd done to London and was greatly relieved to hear my new publisher shout, 'It's a triumph!' At first I thought he must be talking about somebody else. But even I knew that one's first book – I had, it is true, written one shortish essay about the Marsh Arabs called *Return to the Marshes* before this, and it had been well received – was the most important thing in one's life. Except the second, of course, because no one would believe you could write *two* books that were any good, although you might manage *one* by a fluke.

Of all the incidents in *Slow Boats to China*, which are the ones that bring an almost overpowering feeling that I should like to repeat the experience again now?

I think, first, the incident in the Trianon Bar in Alexandria with Fuad

A cow being loaded on to a dhow in Dubai dhow harbour. It looks unhappy – and was, it seemed to me – to have slings put round it and to be swung out between sky and earth. Right: A dhow, which is very much like the one that took me to Karachi and nearly burst into flames en route.

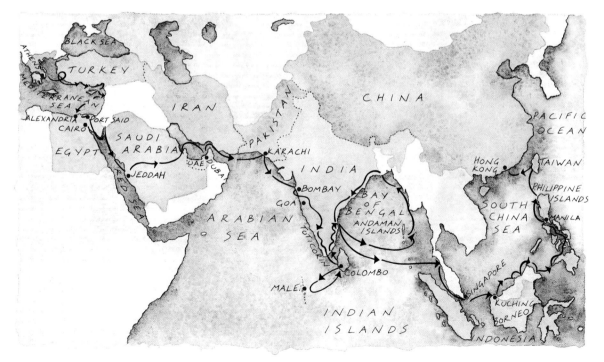

A crew member washing in the 'thunderbox' over the stern of the dhow taking me from Dubai to Karachi.

Bey, the well-dressed but poverty-stricken former horseman and pilot in King Farouk's air force – whose friend had greeted me as I stood admiring the murals there with, 'You should have seen the old tiles they had on the floor. Beautiful.' Fuad, an old gentleman, stood at the marble bar wearing a dark blazer with naval buttons, stiff collar, well-tied wide-knotted tie, light trousers and highly polished shoes and carrying a short malacca cane.

'A nice cane,' I said.

'From Harrods, Brompton Road, SW1, 1926,' he said promptly with a gratified smile. 'I was staying at the Hans Crescent Hotel.'

That was Fuad Bey. What a charming man he was! He was one of the many who had suffered under Nasser. I would like to see him again.

I *have* seen Captain Jean-Noël Visbecq, formerly commander of the *Patrick Vieljeux*. I saw him in St Malo a year or two ago during a conference on travel writing. He looked exactly the same: like a middle-aged actor from the Comédie-Française who should have been wearing seventeenth-century clothes: breeches with ribbons at the knee and a wide lace collar; tall, upright, stately. I would like to thank Captain Visbecq once more for his admirably supportive manner towards me when I was 'attacked' by a malicious Saudi shipping agent in Jeddah.

And I would like to see Captain Ismail Rashad again – the man who could sing like Nat King Cole and who did his best to get me on to a ship through the Suez Canal, and finally succeeded in securing my passage on the *Patrick Vieljeux*. I wonder if he is still alive. I tend to forget that all these things happened a long time ago, although it seems like yesterday.

My memories of the Suez Canal went back much further than the Six Day War of 1967 or the war of 1972, when Sadat's men stormed across the canal into Israel shouting, '*Allahu Akhbar!*' They reach back to my national service, in fact, which I spent in the Welsh Guards just after the Second World War. In 1947 we were posted to the Middle East, Palestine to be exact, and there, I imagine, my adventure lust was born.

I remember the arrival of my army draft at the crossing of the Canal at Ismailyia. In the dead of night on the railway journey up the coast of Palestine to Gaza and Sarafand Arab thieves got on the train with us and perched on the buffers between the carriages. Now and again they pounced and grabbed any webbing belts the guardsmen had left lying close to their thieving hands.

Later, things started looking up in Tiberias with a company commander, Jerry Spencer-Smith, who loved the open air, shooting wildfowl and

The rather ordinary sail of the dhow that took me in the end to Karachi from Dubai.

the Middle East, not necessarily in that order. He allowed us to go on 'safaris' to Jordan, where we stayed with Glubb Pasha's men of the Arab Legion and visited Petra, Jerash and Kerak high in the mountains overlooking the Dead Sea.

At that time my love of the desert, Bedu and all things Arab was born. I went back to Jordan many times later. I got to know Kerak very well indeed and spent several Christmases in Petra in the tent that they put up there for people like me. The Majali family of Kerak became good friends and the Bushnaqs of the Arab Bank in Amman, and many other good and wise Jordanians. When I caught a bad case of hepatitis in Jerusalem, King Hussein himself came to the Palestine Hospital to present me with a *wreath*. I thought I was a goner then, I don't mind saying. But I survived, as you see.

Of course, I have a very soft spot for Khalat, Lal Mohamed, Sumar and all the other jolly Baluchis of the *Al Raza*, which took me from Dubai to Karachi: they were an exceptional lot of men. I keep a specially warm spot in my heart for Captain Beale of the Andaman Islands, the

Richard Wesse, a German who lived in Goa. He was an extraordinary-looking man, 'dressed like a Mississippi gambler in a film, in a white three-piece suit and shoes, very elegant'. For some reason I found him sinister, like Joseph Conrad's Mr Jones in Victory. *In the picture he is standing outside his amazing villa in Goa, the Villa Nunez – not sinister at all; delightful, in fact. He reminded me then of R. L. Stevenson in Western Samoa. Right: Building dhows in Colombo.*

friend of Bala, who was the Indian captain of the *Nancowry* and took me to Port Blair from Madras. Naturally, I shall never forget Captain Beale and his small son Gavin, who is now quite big, I suppose. Or Beale's launch, the *Gavin*, for that matter.

I find I have forgotten to mention Mr Missier of Colombo, who put me on board the *Herman Mary*, the Tamil sailing vessel that took me, with Tom Abraham's help, to India. Mr Missier was the sort of good man one doesn't meet that often any more — although the world seemed full of people like him a few years ago. The last word I received from him was an invitation to his daughter's wedding at St Lucia Cathedral; 'to share' (as the wording of the invitation said) 'their happiness and ours at the solemnization'.

I must mention the *Starling Cook* on the storm-tossed launch that took me to Malé in the Maldives. I was truly frightened on this trip and I remember thinking, What am I doing here? and wishing I was somewhere else — anywhere — on dry land at least. It was the only time I felt despair like that on the whole round-the-world trip.

Part of the crew of the launch that took me to Malé in the Maldives. Right: The crew of the Herman Mary *in action. This was the sailing vessel that took me to Colombo, in Sri Lanka, and on to Tuticorin, in India.*

But, of course, the sailors I most want to meet again in the world are the Filipinos on the kumpit (a launch) that took me from Sandakan to Zamboanga and then sailed on to Cebu without me: the kumpit that was ambushed by Moros in the Sulu Sea. I wonder quite often what has happened to Crazy Jan, the 'Ayatollah', Carlos and Small-But-Terrible. Where are they? I have no idea. I still believe that that adventure with the Moros was the most exciting I ever had during that long sea voyage.

No account of that trip would be complete without a mention of dear old Captain Ralph Kennet of the *Hupeh*. With his repeated talk of 'Nut-megs' and 'Shall I co-mpare thee to a soomer's day?' he livened up the last leg of my trip no end. I see him fairly often in Gloucestershire where he has retired to his 'shed' in Slad – a 'shed', by the way, which has a huge garden and twenty-odd rooms. Ralph lives there quite alone. He has even given up his customary tipple of rum-and-Coke.

So that is that. It is all over now; but it was a great adventure. People still come up to me and ask me about *Slow Boats to China*, although I have written other books that I consider to be better. I have to admit, though, that I enjoy reading *Slow Boats* more than most others; it rein-troduces me to the men and women I once met and loved.

I have to say one thing more. *Slow Boats* introduced me not only to these seamen, but also to my illustrator Salim, who, as I have already said, wanted to go to sea with me and sketch from life. There simply was not enough money for that, alas.

120

Perhaps I, and more spectacularly Paul Theroux, caught a 'trend' early on and were lucky. I don't know. Frankly, I don't waste too much sleep pondering that sort of unanswerable question. I am grateful to people like Hentry and his brother Romans, and Darson, for having shown me that 'thrift, hard work, reverence are the main virtues,' as the poet Philip Larkin said. They were all virtues shared by the crew of the *Herman Mary* between Colombo and Tuticorin. And, as I say in the book, Larkin's 'What will survive of us in love', fitted the sailors of Tuticorin, too.

The main thing I learned from this long voyage was that it was a pleasure, first, to be outside the range of a foreign editor's telephone and, second, that it was a great relief not to have to always be struggling with masses of wounded and miserable refugees, or confronting desolation and destroyed buildings, or always being terrified to death by *someone*'s jets and helicopters. Yet one has to admit that people in wars are usually far more outgoing than elsewhere. It is fear, I suppose, that makes people unwind and reveal themselves in a serious, or even a jokey, way. That is one appeal of war situations. I imagine it was for me, anyway.

Although I no longer had to face the hazards of war, I cannot overstress how much worry I suffered over the possibility of missing the next ship or not being allowed to board her. My passage through the Suez Canal was one of the greatest hazards I faced at that time and I wouldn't like to have to go through all that hassle again, with or without the help of Captain Ismail Rashad. It would not have been the same, for me at least, if I had had to motor down the Canal from Port Said to Suez by road. It was worries like this that made the voyage at times nerveracking. The Saudi shipping agent in Jeddah, for example, did more than simply offend Captain Visbecq, he put the fear of God into me; I had no wish to go to jail in Jeddah – possibly for an indefinite period.

Similarly, I was horrified to discover that the dhow I thought I had arranged to travel on from Dubai had sailed without me; although I was lucky – Lal Mohamed, Khalat and the rest easily made up for that loss in the end. I would not have missed my trip on the 'burning' *Al Raza* for anything.

So there are good and bad elements in every situation. And, on the whole, I would be willing to go through the entire adventure again. That is, without having to write the book. That may have been the hardest part.

Praus in a harbour in the Philippines. The lights probably indicate that this boat was used for night fishing.

Chinese lion dancers preparing their act in a New Year festival in Kuching, Sarawak. They are about to get inside the lion frames and cavort through the streets.

Overleaf: Filipino children waiting on the shore of the island to greet the crew of the **kumpit** *(launch) and myself as we neared Zamboanga.*

Slow Boats Home, the sequel to my previous book, tells the story of my return to Plymouth from the China Seas. One of my favourite parts of the book is the beginning, where I write about Hong Kong and Shanghai. Now, of course, Hong Kong has gone – reunited with 'mother' China on 1 July 1997 – and all I am left with are the words of Tom Dor in a Shanghai restaurant years ago. I remember him saying: 'When the communists came here in 1949 – the day my ills began – the buses ran, I remember. Odd that, but they ran. There was the cheering. And disciplined troops. Until the communists knew what was going on in Shanghai there were few big arrests. Until 1951, I guess. Cabarets went on. Prostitution even. I remember the buses going round the streets one night much later. Rounding up the prostitutes, for rehabilitation!'

Various people, Chinese as well as expatriates, have predicted that it will take the communist leadership in Beijing some time to 'know all about' Hong Kong. They think there are unlikely to be any 'big arrests' until 1999, if things go there as they went in Shanghai in 1949. We shall see.

'Shanghai,' Thomas Dor sighed, 'could be really fine, but,' he added, 'the communists must always *interfere* – that's the trouble.' These words also made me think of Hong Kong and feel sad. Again, we shall see.

Over the years I have seen my friends So Wei Kuen and Ah Po many times in Hong Kong. So Wei Kuen has changed jobs since I first met him: he is no longer driving a fork-lift truck for Esso, he is in construction work; and so is Ah Po. Ah Po, in early middle age, has begun to go bald on the very top of his head – although only someone as tall as I am can see that – otherwise he is still smiling that same gormless and charming smile, and still unable to speak a word of English; well, hardly a word. Ah Po's daughter is taller than he is now and very beautiful. I used to think that one day she might marry So Wei Kuen's son, who is now also a bean-pole, but not nearly so attractive, I'm afraid. So that will probably not happen. So Wei Kuen is worried now about the hand-over to China, but there is nothing he or Ah Po can do about it. In any case, Ah Po is indifferent to the whole process; it is above him, he says.

Hangchow was one Chinese port I particularly wanted to visit. I had made a promise to go there assuming 'with childish logic' that Cheeko, my grandfather's chow dog with the regrettable impulse to chase sheep, had been born in Hangchow, or that at least his forebears had.

I never made it to Hangchow; more's the pity. Instead I found a Swire ship in Hong Kong just setting off to the Solomon Islands via Papua

Above: A Bougainville beauty.

Right: A small crowd of children in the Solomon Islands. Occasionally Solomon Islanders have strikingly blond curly hair. Below: Colson with his tam-o'-shanter at the harbour of Guadalcanal.

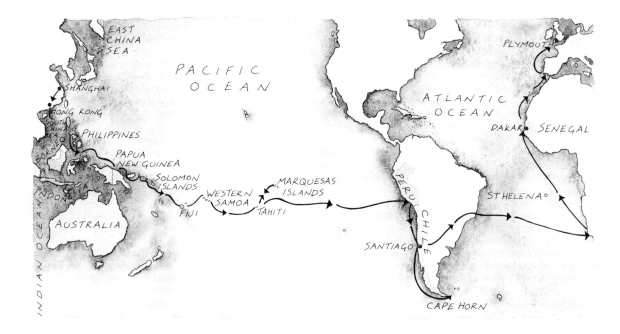

New Guinea, which I longed to visit; so for once I was in the right place at the right time. I had also acquired a battered copy of an old book, *Isles of Illusion*, by the man whose pseudonym 'Asterisk' hid his true identity, which was Fletcher, a schoolmaster who ended his days at tiny St Petroc's school in Bude that, by chance, happened to be just down the road from where I had been brought up in Ocean View Road in that obscure seaside town in Cornwall.

So I set off with the *Chengtu*: happy, at last, to be going in the right direction – across the Pacific Ocean – and on time, too. The trip to Shanghai had taken a very short time but it had been well worthwhile. Without it, I would never have met So Wei Kuen and Ah Po or Mr Shi, my official guide.

I wonder what happened to Colson, the Solomon Islander with the atomic hairdo? Referring to himself as 'a poor lost guy' on finding work

A farmer on Nuku Hiva
(in the Marquesas) and
his mule loaded with
bananas. Right: The
view from Gauguin's and
Jacques Brel's tombs in
Nuku Hiva. I clambered
about the tombs and
found Gauguin's name
written on a stone near a
statue of the Tahitian
god/goddess Oviri.

in Gizo, he later wrote to me saying that everything was 'in good condition. Except poor, poor beautiful me! Getting all hot and scratched by wood branches. Penniless, hopeless, all alone in the world.' He had signed the letter, 'Your everlasting friend, Irish Colson (The Lost Guy).' But what could I do about it? All that was in 1982, which is fifteen years ago as I write this. 'You must come back,' Colson had written then, but if I went back how would I find him? He had started the letter, 'Dearest G. Young', so perhaps I should make an effort to find him again.

As for Tolu, Fili, Amosa, Isaia and Emma, I would dearly love to see them all again. But Western Samoa is a long way off. I have been back once to visit them – and sadly found that Amosa was fat (Samoans don't remain slim long), and Emma had gone off to New Zealand. Fili, too, had grown huge; only Isaia had remained himself. Tolu wanted me to stay and become a village chief near his place. But when I asked Alan Gray at the hotel about it he said, 'No. On no account. Don't think about it. It's not worth it.' So I took his advice, having had no one else's to take. But, still, of all the places in the Pacific I just *might* return to, Western Samoa is the place, Apia is the town and Tiavaea is the village.

I nearly got myself stranded with no boat to take me any further than Tahiti. I was saved by a Russian cruise ship, the *Alexander Pushkin*, which eventually appeared to take me on to Callao in Peru. It was a

nasty moment; the thought of being stuck halfway across the Pacific Ocean for months with no boats at all going my way – all the cargo ships seemed to be going east to west and I, of course, wanted to go west to east. I had to break a rule and take a cruise ship to get out of Tahiti, but it was worth it just to meet and become friendly with Eric Hart – I compared him to a mixture of Lord Carrington and Mr McGoo, the cartoon character. Eric was in charge of the ship's on-shore visits. He and I, being the only two Englishmen aboard the *Alexander Pushkin* – with the exception of a singer and a conjurer – were able to stick together when the West German geriatrics, to whom the vessel was leased apparently, ganged up on the British (us) in defence of the Argies, for whom they evidently felt some affection. Luckily, there were also some Dutch passengers aboard who didn't agree with them. But there was a period when Eric and I were deliberately led to believe that the British expeditionary force was in dire trouble and the government of Maggie Thatcher might fall. We survived, however, and soon made it from Callao to the British Embassy in Lima where the true picture – a victorious one – was presented to us. And then, while Eric sailed away on the *Alexander Pushkin* – I was to see him later in England many times – I went on down to friendly Chile where there was no love lost for the Argentines; Peru, by the way, had been very pro-Argentine (someone had even put a bomb near the embassy doors, the ambassador told Eric and me).

Chile provided me with a fantastic adventure – a visit to the island of Cape Horn in midwinter. The man responsible for that was Hernan Cubillos, an ex-foreign minister of Chile, a fine and enthusiastic yachtsman and first-class businessman. Hernan was closely connected to the Chilean navy, for some reason that escapes me, and they were in sympathy with Great Britain, again for some reason that escapes me (but I think it had something to do with the founder of the Chilean navy, Lord Cochrane). At any rate, Hernan prevailed upon the senior naval officers at Puerto Williams to let me land on the island of Cape Horn in midwinter. And I spent a glorious three days there, with a handful of Chilean marines who were based in this wild, wind-swept and frozen outpost, expecting to be attacked by the Argies. I shall never forget the contempt and hatred the Chileans felt for the Argentines, or the moment when Menendez, the engineer, said to me, 'Nuñez, the marine sergeant, wants to say that before today the Chilean navy had one saint – Santa Carmen – but from now on the navy has *two* saints. The second saint is Santa Margarita.'

'Saint Margaret?'

'*Sí*! Santa Margarita *Thatcher*.'

'Hey – Santa Margarita!' cried Osorio, patting my shoulder. '*Bueno!*'

That was a high spot, but it was followed by a very low spot off the coast of Brazil. There I found a South African ship which had a very chequered career after I joined her. For a start, there was a mutiny; the Zulu crew of that ship, which I called the *Piranha* in my book, mutinied against the white officers, particularly objecting to the chief officer, an enormous man with glasses, whom they all cordially disliked because they said he was trying to take over the running of the ship despite the presence of an easy-going but toughish Dutch captain. In the end, the ship lost its rudder backing on to a pinnacle of rock and its ability to go anywhere, and I left her – without sorrow – to fly to Rio and thence to Cape Town from where I took a ship to St Helena and the Falklands, and from there, with diversions, to Plymouth. From Rio my way was plain sailing, and from there to Plymouth (which was 'Home') all went well.

I arrived in Plymouth on the old *Kaina* with a fine group of seamen – Tom Newby, the delightful skipper, was an old hand, just come along to keep his hand in on the bridge, and was about to retire once more to his home near Cardiff's Tiger Bay. Keith and Frank were a couple of 'old lags' (if seamen can be called that), and I loved them both. They reminded me of two characters in a short story by W. W. Jacobs.

So many fine people – many never seen again. So many strange faces and nationalities never revisited. It was a good thing to have done those voyages; I have no doubt of that. But I have deep regrets when I read my own books now. Sometimes I wonder: couldn't I have visited *some* of those places, ships and people just once more?

But even if I had, I should probably *still* have been left wondering, could I – *should* I – go back once more?

That way nothing lies but permanent regret. One more time . . . one more time . . . and then, what? The same nagging ache of failed duty, of *regret*. What is one to do? The only thing to do is to be glad one made the most of those opportunities. To rejoice that one took those opportunities; that is all.

A Senegalese lady dressed to kill, with her child. We stopped off at a small port on the West African coast; they were selling fish there.

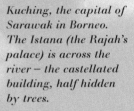

Kuching, the capital of Sarawak in Borneo. The Istana (the Rajah's palace) is across the river – the castellated building, half hidden by trees.

1977 In Search of Conrad

Joseph Conrad may not have been to Sarawak in the flesh, but he was certainly there in spirit. His admiration for James Brooke, the first white rajah of that romantic place on the coast of Borneo, knew no bounds. The setting of Kuching, its capital, is Conradian in its extreme drama, too, and the Istana (Palace) of the Rajah Brookes stands on the river bank opposite the main body of the city, brooding there like some building from a nineteenth-century book of old prints.

Tom Lingard of the novels (William Lingard in real life) was modelled on James Brooke. Conrad wrote in one passage:

there were others – obscure adventurers who had not [Brooke's] advantages of birth, position and intelligence; who had only his sympathy with the people of forests and sea he understood and loved so well. They can not be said to be forgotten since they have not been known at all. They were lost in the common crowd of seamen-traders of the Archipelago.

One such man *par excellence* was William Lingard. 'People like him,' wrote Conrad, 'have tinged with romance the region of shallow waters and forest-clad islands that lie far east and still mysterious between the deep waters of two oceans.'

The passing countryside of Celebes (Sulawesi) had a calming effect on one, like myself, who was fed up with the bombs, shelling and noise of the helicopters in the wars of Vietnam and elsewhere. Whether it was of quiet peasant goings-on on shore (above) or tranquil boats on the rivers (below).

Fiona – she had been built in Poole, Dorset, in England, in 1912, so she was no longer in her first youth.

*My old friend Wilfred
Thesiger was aboard.*

The Conrad novels in which Lingard figures include *An Outcast of the Islands* and *Almayer's Folly*. *Lord Jim* deals with the same river 'upstream by about 40 miles' that saw Lingard & Co.'s offices erected with Almayer installed there as Lingard's agent until Lingard was ousted from his leading role as Berau-trader by the Singapore Arabs with their steamers.

I had been obsessed with the works of Joseph Conrad since I was a boy in Bude in Cornwall. As I have already mentioned, I was brought up in my grandmother's house, that had a distant view of the sea – you could just see a half-moon of sea water between the roofs if you stood in an upstairs room and craned out of the round window, I remember. The bookshelves downstairs were lined with books by Conrad and Kipling; I can see their blue bindings still and the gold lettering that gave their fascinating names: *The Nigger of the Narcissus*, *Typhoon* and the rest. My father, who was in the regular army but was really a sailor *manqué*, died aged eighty with a copy of *The Mirror of the Sea* at his bedside.

When I became a war correspondent, I took to carrying a copy of a Conrad novel with me both as a sort of talisman and also as a reminder that my hectic life was probably on the right track; that is, the one that *Youth* had pointed out to me. It was a reading from *Youth*, that dramatic piece of fiction based on Conrad's life, that inspired me to travel in the first place.

I need not tell you what it is to be knocking about in an open boat. I remember nights and days of calm when we pulled, we pulled, and the boat seemed to stand still, as if bewitched within the circle of the sea horizon. I remember the heat, the deluge of rain-squalls that kept us baling for dear life (but filled our water-cask), and I remember sixteen hours on end with a mouth dry as a cinder and a steering-oar over the stern to keep my first command head on to a breaking sea. I did not know what a good man I was till then. I remember the drawn faces, the dejected figures of my two men, and I remember my youth and the feeling that will never come back any more – the feeling that I could last for ever, outlast the sea, the earth, and all men; the deceitful feeling that lures us on to joys, to perils, to love, to vain effort – to death; the triumphant conviction of strength, the heat of life in the handful of dust, the glow in the heart that with every year grows dim, grows cold, grows small, and expires, too soon, too soon – before life itself.

I have written that my war reporting took me to the Congo and Katanga, the scene of Conrad's *Heart of Darkness*. And several other places I visited: Bangkok, for example; Borneo and Singapore had led me to begin to 'see' the world of Conrad's novels. I began to feel I was surrounded by spectres from *Lord Jim* and *Victory*. In Singapore or Bangkok, I would catch the flick of Marlowe's nautical jacket or a whiff of his cheroot, or get a glimpse of Captain Whalley's bushy whiskers on Singapore's sunlit Esplanade.

I began my search for Joseph Conrad in the 42-foot ketch *Fiona*, with my old friend Wilfred Thesiger aboard (I thought I owed him something for introducing me to the Marsh Arabs all those years ago) and my godson Murray Moncrief, who was something of a sailor. And, of course, Mac, *Fiona*'s owner and skipper. *Fiona* herself had been built in Poole, England, in 1912, so she was no longer in her first youth. But she was good all through, had her original masts, a huge main cabin and an engine.

As a matter of fact, my search for Conrad's world took place in two widely spaced parts, one in 1977 in *Fiona*, the other eleven years later, in 1988, in what are called 'country boats', that took me from Samarinda to Tanjung Redeb, the place where the fictional Lord Jim got his comeuppance, and Almayer was betrayed (as he thought) by Tom Lingard. This made my book a very tricky one to put together because there was Conrad's story to deal with and a great deal of my story. But, thank the Lord, it was finally done and the book was called *In Search of Conrad*

Some Indonesian men wore costumes that were good-looking in the extreme. I met this man in Rangas, a small port on the west coast of the central Celebes.

Opposite above: A prau harbour in Kambunong, a small port a few miles north of Rangas. Below: The graveyard in Gowa, just south of Makassar in the Celebes. This was the final resting-place of the ancient kings. The roofs are daubed with graffiti and the place reminded me of Dracula.

(I still think the French version had a better title; it was *The Ghosts of Joseph Conrad*).

Still, there was a degree of tranquillity in my life while I was writing my books which had been missing before. Graham Greene has said somewhere that a writer is always living on his nerves. That is certainly true of a war correspondent. Apart from the actual dangers of the war situation, there is the continual struggle to get copy to the home base in time for the next edition. That worry is eliminated in book-writing. There is nowhere near such a tight deadline. So the nerve-factor simply disappears.

Also the passing countryside had a calming effect on me – whether it was quiet peasant goings-on on shore or tranquil sailing ships or boats on the rivers around one. Some of the Indonesian men and their costumes were good-looking to the extreme – and that, too, had a soothing effect. The moonlight on a jungle rooftop or pagoda or temple had an enchantment of its own; as far removed as possible from the lethal crash of mortar bombs or the ear-splitting racket of helicopters.

I'm sure Islam had something to do with the calmness of the people we met; and also much of the rapacity of certain officials, I'm afraid. But it had on the whole a beneficial effect, I think. It is an odd thing, but true, that Indonesian policemen, whose job it is to regulate the modalities of life, are often the most unscrupulous and rapacious of all the people one is likely to meet. Is this chance, I wonder? On the other hand, some of the *bupatis* (the civilian minor governors or harbour masters) in the small ports we visited were among the most generous and honest people we met on the entire expedition. It was strange. We never managed to get to the bottom of this enigma.

It is surprising and gratifying to find just how much of Conrad's world has remained unchanged; has stayed, that is to say, as Conrad left it. That was another plus for me.

Singapore, on the other hand, has changed a great deal; there has been a determined effort to pull down its past and rebuild it as a new Hong Kong; a modern skyscraper city that looks like any modern city anywhere in the world. But I found that Conrad survives even here. True, the Malabar Hotel he frequented – the Hotel de l'Europe – has been replaced by the Supreme Court, and Raffles Hotel – which in any case he was far too busy and too poor to enter – is now more an expensive museum than an expensive hostelry. But the National Library still

holds the world of Conrad in its files, and Lilly Tan, the dedicated lady at the National Archives, is still as committed as ever to bringing the past to life.

Reclamation and rebuilding have been the ruin of so much of Singapore's past that it *is* difficult to resurrect it; but that it can still be done I hope I have shown. The same, of course, goes for Bangkok, which has become a byword for pollution and traffic jams and whose skyline gets more and more cluttered with skyscrapers every year. But the temples are still there and remain indestructible (literally), and the Chao Phraya River is still, as always, the Spirit of Thailand, so it is possible to gather together Conrad's world there effectively enough.

As for Indonesia, that country is the most redolent of Conrad's world. Of course, you might still find the grave of Austin Williams (the original Lord Jim) in the Bididari cemetery in Singapore – if you are lucky and have patience; but Surabaya in Java and Makassar (now called Ujung Pandang) in Celebes (now called Sulawesi) are unchanged more or less. This goes too for the smaller places: the Bugis lands of Celebes and

A river scene at sunset – very near where Almayer (or Olmeijer) lived and Lord Jim died in Tanjung Redeb, Borneo.

the upper reaches of the Bulungan and Berau rivers, which are still relatively unexplored since Lingard put Almayer (or Olmeijer) there as his agent to buy from the Dyaks the quantities of rattans, gutta percha and bird's nests that made him rich in the nineteenth century.

Then there is Bangka Island. I was initially drawn there, or to Muntok, its port, not because Muntok is beautiful — it is not — but by Conrad's autobiographical story, *Youth*. In this book Conrad's ship blows up near the Gaspar Strait in Indonesia, and the young Conrad finds that his first 'command' was in charge of a lifeboatful of a handful of seamen who had to pull like the devil at the oars to get them safe to shore — at Muntok.

I sailed to Muntok in the Indonesian ship *Lawit* and saw it almost exactly as Conrad had seen it a hundred years before. Across the big, shallow bay I could see a long sweep of beach ending in a prominent white lighthouse. It had been night when the survivors of the *Palestine* (Conrad's ship) had reached this bay; they saw the outline of mountains, the beach gleaming in the dark, and dimly made out the light at the end of the wharf and steered for it.

Even from a mile away in daylight the shore looked surprisingly unpopulated. It was an exciting moment. I could see a few roofs half hidden among trees, two longish ramshackle buildings where the *Lawit*'s captain said tin was processed for export, one or two godowns and a spindly iron-strutted jetty. And that was all.

One night a hundred years ago, a disembodied cry had rung out across this patch of water: 'What steamer is this, pray?' — the voice of Second Officer Conrad Korzeniowski, fatigue emphasizing his thick Polish accent.

I had arrived at Muntok, the port of Bangka Island.

Bangka happened also to be the home of Freya, the lover of chestnut-haired Jasper Allen of the pretty brig *Bonito*. Freya's piano-playing — Wagner mostly — drove her bumbling old father Nielson (or Nelson) to senility and death from a broken heart in Bayswater. But the fate of Allen was far worse; he was ruined and reduced to penury by the spiteful actions of a Dutch officer called Heemskirk. Freya had already died of love for Allen — or was it merely pneumonia in wintry Hong Kong? So Bangka was the home of Conrad's *Freya of the Seven Isles*, a tragic story. It was certainly another reason for going there.

I must warn you – if you are a determined Joseph Conrad-seeker –
that the average Indonesian has never heard of Conrad or Lingard or
Olmeijer (or Almayer). But never mind: we have a secret, you and I; we
know they existed and we know where their ghosts are to be found. That
should be enough for us. That, and the beautiful seas and rivers, the
reefs and the jungle, which remain, more or less, just as Conrad left
them.

Tribal dancers. Samburu tribesmen love dancing and part of their routine consists of leaping high into the air.

1979 Kenya

Shortly before I embarked on the first of my ships at Piraeus for *Slow Boats to China*, I went to visit my old friend Wilfred Thesiger in Kenya, where he was then living. It was also after I had taken him on the ketch *Fiona* on the first leg of my voyages to recapture Joseph Conrad's past for *In Search of Conrad*. As I have already said, I wanted to repay Wilfred, one of whose favourite books was Conrad's *Lord Jim*, for having provided me with one of the first and finest adventures of my life: the visit to the Marsh Arabs.

'It'll end in tears, you mark my words,' said one of Wilfred's friends when he heard of our projected voyage in *Fiona*. But it didn't; it ended in smiles and laughter all round. So did my visit to Kenya.

Wilfred was then sixty-nine, but I remember remarking that he looked ten years younger. His hard brown face still looked like a splinter of knotty wood; his oddly long nose still had curious kinks in it, the mementoes of four years of being undefeated light heavyweight champion of Oxford University. He still looked like a print out of one of those old books of exploration by Mungo Park of Africa or Charles Doughty or Richard Burton of Arabia. If he had been born in 1836 – the year he would have chosen – he would have been the respected colleague of all those men.

The 'respected colleague': not necessarily the 'ideal travelling companion'. Wilfred has the prima donna's sharp tongue. Still, he has been awarded all the prizes for travelling one can think of: the Founder's Medal of the Royal Geographical Society; the Lawrence of Arabia Medal of the Royal Central Ocean Society; the Livingstone Medal of the Royal Scottish Geographical Society; the Burton Medal of the Royal Oceanic Society. Add to that two books, *Arabian Sands* and *The Marsh Arabs*, a Fellowship of the Royal Society of Literature, and a couple of marvellous books of photographs, and you realize he's not done too badly for a man who jokes that he's never done a stroke of work in his life.

There are other things that might surprise you about Wilfred Thesiger. For instance, you would hardly expect to find him, pushing seventy, last from the Victorian mould of great explorers, close to fisticuffs up a side-street in sw3. But you would be wrong.

I found him once, a tall, tanned figure, not unlike Sherlock Holmes, dressed in an old-fashioned suit and waistcoat with a gold watch-chain and carrying an elderly umbrella, progressing down Paradise Walk with the long, flat-footed strides so well remembered by the countless tribesmen from Kashgar to Arabia's Empty Quarter who have struggled to keep up with him. At the bottom of the street a number of motorists had been blocked in by a bull-necked man of about thirty-six at the wheel of a large car. Amid the cursing and hooting, Thesiger asked the angry man, with the quiet courtesy of a bygone age, if he could help him to reverse the six feet necessary to let others pass.

The reply was explosive. 'Je-e-e-sus Chri-i-st! How I *hate* the upper classes!' the man yelled, and when Thesiger repeated his offer ('The car was far grander than anything I or my friends could afford in a thousand years,' he later told me), the man fumbled with his door, muttering, 'Right – I'm going to break your f— neck . . .!'

It was, said Thesiger later, a lovely prospect. He put a long, hard hand on the door handle. 'I'll help you get out,' he said mildly, 'but I should warn you that you will get hurt.' Deep, pale eyes under shaggy eyebrows stared as blankly and steadily at the angry man in the car as they had gazed over a rifle's sights at lion in the Sudan and wild boar in Iraq. Crashing his gears, the man drove apoplectically away. And Thesiger was soon round the corner in his small sitting room lined with African

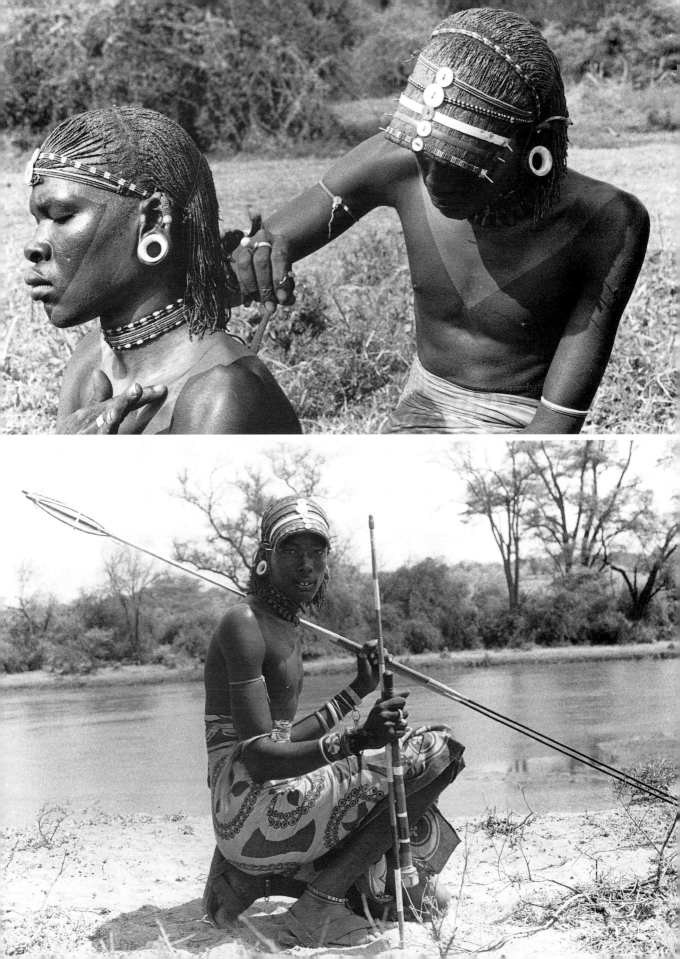

A young Kenyan would-be warrior. The feathered headdress mean he is about to be circumcised and become a warrior.

and Arabian first editions and hung with Arab daggers, plaintively sighing over a cup of Earl Grey to his devoted housekeeper, Miss Emtage: 'The bloody man funked it!'

That's just another side of Thesiger.

At Nairobi airport we are met by Lawi and some of Thesiger's other African friends. Lawi was a friend *par excellence* – one of those precious people who seem endowed with an extra ration of warmth and sense of goodness. He was then twenty-six, tall, quick-witted, humorous, amazingly good-natured. He was a first-class driver-mechanic; a natural rock-climber, and a good boxer in the classical style (taught by Thesiger). 'In fact,' said Thesiger to tease him, 'there's very little you are not – in your own estimation, Lawi.'

'Now then, *mzee juu*, don't be unkind like dees.' *Mzee juu* means 'top elder', a term of particular respect. Thesiger was addressed as *mzee juu* by nearly all the tribesmen we met in northern Kenya.

Poor Lawi is now dead, alas. He went into politics, took to the bottle, and died quite young of cirrhosis of the liver. Thesiger even now has not quite got over that blow. He returned to London from Kenya quite soon after and now lives in Chelsea. He himself has never drunk a drop of the hard stuff, although, from time to time, I have seen him sipping a small glass of something sweet, like Drambuie.

When I was with him in Kenya Thesiger lived very frugally. I tried in a piece I sent to *The Observer* to compare the African lifestyles of Ernest Hemingway (as he portrayed them in his novels, at least) and Thesiger's. I said that the camp Thesiger made every evening was basic. 'Bring whisky-soda for the *memsahib*,' is Hemingway, not Thesiger. Women in jodhpurs who drink too much and are handy in bed with white hunters and own houses on Fifth Avenue – that's Hemingway, not Thesiger. Hemingway's world is a world of ice-boxes, chairs, tables, collapsible wash-basins and canvas cooling-bags. A world in which African bearers are sent to camp 200 yards downwind. Not Thesiger's world at all.

In Thesiger's world, under huge spreading trees between rocky hills, someone puts water on the fire for tea. We unpack: a sack of maize and a battered Blue Band butter carton containing Oxo cubes, packet soups, onions, potatoes, mugs, spoons (no forks or knives), tea, sugar; one paraffin lamp; metal cooking pots and a frying pan; plastic bowls; cheap torches with broken bulbs; *pangas* and a spade; loo paper; Thesiger's towel and sponge bag.

Typical tribal women at the door of their house in northern Kenya. One is holding her baby.

Two tribesmen washing in a stream in northern Kenya. Right: Close-up of a painted Samburu tribesman in northern Kenya.

We buy a goat from small herd-boys who emerge cautiously from the bush, and while Lawi is skinning our one meal a day, I remember Wilfred in those Marsh days. I still see a tall figure squelching briskly through mud and reed stubble. Huge wild boar lurk ahead. Thesiger is in a tweed jacket, is barefoot, has tucked his Arab ankle-length shirt under his belt and thus has exposed hugely muscled calves and baggy knee-length drawers. He looks like a cross between the ultimate Great White Hunter and Widow Twankey.

We drink Twining's Earl Grey at the fire. 'America has nothing like this,' said Thesiger. 'As for you, Lawi, I suppose some people would call you Kipling's bloody 'eathen, wouldn't they?'

Lawi laughed. '*Mzee juu*, you know I'm a Catholic.'

'Well, I'm an atheist, so I'm the bloody 'eathen,' said Thesiger. 'Lawi, don't forget, when I die I want my corpse laid out in the bush for the hyenas. I mean that.'

'Anything you weesh, *mzee juu*,' said Lawi, fondly.

But time has passed. And, alas, Lawi will not be laying anyone's corpse out in the bush any more.

1993 Yukon

The English poet Robert Service wrote memorably about the Yukon River and the Klondike during the Gold Rush at the turn of the last century. All about Dangerous Dan McGrew and the Malamute Saloon, and a bunch of the boys who, he said, were whooping it up there.

When I arrived in Dawson City in 1993, in a temperature of 50° below zero, the Malamute Saloon had become known as the Snake Pit Bar and was a fine place for the boys, who had been whooping it up there for some time by the look of things. They wore beards and bearskin coats and sat in a haze of cigarette smoke and whisky fumes. A four-piece band was playing Turkey-in-the-Straw type music: including an Indian fiddler from Yellowknife on the Great Slave Lake, a pianist in a bowler hat, and a guitarist from God knows where; some raucous people were tipsily dancing on a minute square of floor in one corner.

It was, I thought, a typical Dawson City winter scene. In fact, the Malamute Saloon (a Malamute is a large husky dog from the Bering Strait of Alaska) never existed, so the Snake Pit Bar was the next best thing.

I had just returned to celebrate the Thaw – the time when the Yukon River begins to melt and the world becomes once more a green place and things *flow* again – from the trapper's hut of Paul Wylie and his wife, 40 miles north of Dawson, where Wylie and his wife lived all the year round with their twenty-one huskies: big animals, 100 lb on average, said Paul, who believes that the bigger the dogs the more intelligent they are.

The dog sleigh. The huskies are ready to tumble me in the snow.

Paul Wylie outside his snow-covered hut on the Forty Mile River. With him is his lead dog. Right: A car outside the Westminster Hotel, Dawson City — otherwise known as the Snake Pit Bar. It was a great place to be at 50° below zero.

The dogs were intelligent, all right; in fact, I found them too intelligent. They took one crafty look at me and on the spot decided I was just the sort of visitor that was worth dumping. The sport of 'dumping' means throwing the human being off the sled the dogs are drawing into *deep* snow. And it is done by heading at speed for a good turning-place, and quickly shooting off to the left or right so that the human driver (who is standing on the far back-end of the long, heavy sled) has no alternative but to throw himself off the sled into deep snow. It takes, I may say, a very long time to clamber out of snow several feet deep, and meanwhile the dogs have carried on at their leisure to sit down further up the track and rest while you are struggling to regain your upright

position and hobble after them. The dogs, when one catches up with them, would (I swear) be grinning at you. And at once they put their heads together and begin planning the next 'dumping'.

In the end I became friends with the leaders of the dog team and so all was saved. But it took some time and some maddening tumbles. Nothing I had read in Jack London had prepared me for 'dumping'. And Paul, my guide and host, had said nothing to warn me about it. Not out of enmity, he swore. It just hadn't crossed his mind.

So the visit to the Snake Pit Bar was a celebration — for me, at least — of two things: an absence of 'dumping'; and the Thaw-de-Gras, as they called it there.

1996 Return to Vietnam

One of the royal tombs at Hué. This one is the art-deco creation of Khai Dinh, the father of Bao Dai, the last emperor.

Going back to Vietnam was always going to be a great relief. I found Saigon peaceful at last; the police state horrors ended; I could go anywhere and do anything. It was heaven of a sort.

The theatre, I noticed, was featuring a star called Elvis Cong (although what he did I have no idea). I was staying in a new government hotel behind the old Continentale called the Asian Hotel, which was not cheap – although it was not one of the most expensive, like the Continentale itself, where The Continental Shelf (the open terrace) had been glassed in and turned into an Italian restaurant.

Soon I left for Hué. There, after all, was where my story in this country had started. I saw Mme Bong's house – still standing – and the bridges, the river, the market and the citadel (still scarred from the Tet offensive of 1968). And the tombs.

The garden tombs of Hué – the royal tombs of Minh Mang and Tu Duc, Khai Dinh and other former emperors – were always dear to me. I had visited them often. The first time, I think, was in 1965 with Minh and Qué, and I went several times after that. The tombs were elaborate and surrounded by ornamental ponds that were full of large open lotus buds, and lilies, often pink-red blooms on a single long stalk, which looked, I always thought, like flamingos sleeping. Trees and flowers surrounded the ponds – spreading cedars and frangipani, thick grasses and straggling bushes with rust-coloured leaves.

One day an old guide, a survivor, I suppose, from the days of real peace, led us round. He looked like an ancient mandarin in his solar topee, wide cotton pants and a long, shift-like garment buttoned at the neck: a figure from the past.

To me, the peace that reigned so blissfully among these vivid green fields, the water, the temples and royal tombs of Annam, was something much nearer the essence of Vietnam than anything the ideological loudspeaker vans of Hanoi and Saigon could speak of. There was something indescribably valuable here, conveying, I believed – and

The boat that took Tam and myself round Ha Long Bay, the North Vietnamese beauty spot on the extreme northern coast, above Haiphong.

still fervently believe – to all the Madame Bongs, the Minhs and Qués: 'Peace and common sense are all that matter. Peace and conciliation *mean* common sense. All the rest, all the ferocious babble, all the ideological talk from North or South, is a corruption.'

The tomb of Khai Dinh was my favourite – possibly because of its art-deco design, but also because of its sheer beauty. In 1996 I took my driver, Mr Ha – the one who had driven me to Quang Tri – to Hué and bought him a T-shirt. He agreed with me, perhaps because of the T-shirt, I don't know. I had returned there once in the ten years after the war, when the die-hard communists were really in control and when the country was full of malice and economic decay. Then I had gone with Mr Thai, my communist 'minder', which was not the best way to visit. In fact, it was a deeply depressing mistake. I also managed to visit Mme Bong's house in 103 Tran Hung Dao Street by plunging into it suddenly and dragging Mr Thai with me. I found Mme Bong there. She was soon in tears; the first time I had ever seen such a thing, and I was so moved by the sight that I cut the meeting short. But it made me realize that the war had left feelings of a terrible Orwellian dread. Minh and Qué, for example, had done seven years or more in re-education camps; seven years hard labour. They were now in Saigon, I learned, trying desperately to find work and to educate their children.

Mme Bong's house was easier to see after ten years when I was finally able to go back freely as a tourist. I visited the house and found it unchanged – except that it seemed to have got smaller; it had been taken over by someone in local government and a wall had been built dividing it so that the mortar-shell hole in the cement floor had gone. So had the upper floor, as far as I could see. It had never been a grand house; it certainly wasn't one now.

Mme Bong had moved to Saigon, into an even smaller house than the one in Hué. I went to see her there. It was quite easy to go now, easy even to telephone. When I took her photograph in 1997, she looked smaller somehow, and she insisted on putting on her glasses. She dressed up in a plush *ao dai*, which she had never done before – although she took it off as soon as the photograph was taken and replaced it with her usual white cotton one. I had noticed to my dismay that she was going blind and deaf. Phuc, Qué's brother, called there now and again, and Mme Bong arranged that he should accompany me to Hué so that I could revisit her son Van's tomb at Nui Binh.

Phuc came with me, and because, unlike Qué, he speaks reasonable

View of Ha Long Bay.

English he proved very useful. He also knew the site of Van's tomb, which had been moved by the communists in the early 1980s.

While we were at Van's tomb I happened to mention there was a tomb near by that looked familiar; Phuc identified it at once as belonging to Mme Bong's brother, an old man who had quite recently died in Qui Nhon. Ha then drove us to Nui Binh. We went twice; the second time with Thien, Mme Bong's cousin, whom I had last seen in 1972 when he deserted his parachute regiment in Laos and returned to Hué clinging to the undercarriage of a South Vietnamese helicopter. Thien brought his wife, Chi, and his 22-year-old son Dat.

I went on north after that – to Hanoi, in fact, where Tam, my tourist guide friend from Saigon, proposed to show me the local beauty spot called Ha Long Bay.

Ha Long Bay is a strange, perhaps unique, place: a long area of

Mme Bong's house in Hué after the war. The tailors have gone, and the counters that form the front of the house are now stacked with videos and watches. It was never a big house and the new occupants have divided the interior with a wall so that now it is even smaller. Also the upstairs seems to have disappeared.

Mme Bong herself in 1997 in her small house in Saigon. She wore glasses for this picture and an uncharacteristically gaudy ao dai; and she seems to have shrunk.

seashore with occasional great shafts of rock thrusting up out of the water in pillars, some teethlike in shape, some like roman noses, some like limestone rocks that had been simply pushed up from the seabed in a way that I had not seen before – although such a phenomenon exists, on a much smaller scale, I'm told, at Krabi in Thailand. Some of the pillars in Ha Long Bay have caves bored into them by the sea and you can climb up and into them using steps cut into the rock.

Tam was content – and so was I – to buy shrimps for lunch, so fresh that they wriggled in the water of the bowl they came in, and bottled

Phuc (Qué's brother) and myself at Van's tomb at Nui Binh on the outskirts of Hué.

ice-cold beer. We stayed in the Suoimo Hotel, which must have been a hangover from the old days of the Vietnamese domination by Soviet Russia in the late 1970s or early 1980s because it had 'Regulations for Guests' in Russian pinned up in prominent places by each door, and was (quite rightly) rather cheap. The next time I went back there was a grand, new hotel called the Heritage, I think, which was very expensive but rather bleak, and I began to yearn for the older hotel. Even so, the visit to Ha Long Bay meant that I had driven by car all the way from Ca Mau in the South to Ha Long in the North, almost the entire length of Vietnam.

I had already been with Tam and her husband Viet to the Delta, where once again the extraordinary feeling of unaccustomed peace had struck me: the absence of helicopters, jets, shelling and the endless wartime noise of machine guns blasting away in the middle-distance.

We had been to Can Tho to see Tam's family, and later to Chau Doc, where I had made an expedition through a complicated network of canals to see where Mme Bong's small nephews, Ly and Bao, had made their escape through Cambodia into Thailand in 1986. They had been young then – about eighteen and twelve, I think. Now there was nothing to fear; then there certainly *had* been, even though they had paid their bribes to the police. You never knew when a policeman would turn nasty and refuse to honour his – after all, shady – agreement with you. Now Ly and Bao are in the United States, in Virginia, near Washington DC. It was strange to think of them there; safe at last, but in a foreign country. While here I sat in the Delta of Vietnam, happy to be there.

It had been strange – and thrilling – to be back in Saigon again; a place I had spent so much time in twenty or thirty years before. Of course it had changed a good bit. Like a ghost, one had to find one's way through a jungle of new houses and altered rooms, realizing, as someone else has said, that concrete and steel can proliferate like vegetation.

My hotel, the Asian, was in a most familiar neighbourhood in what years ago had been called Tu Do Street and, before that, in French times, Rue Catinat. Now it was Dong Khoi Street. Down the road was the Givral Coffee House, where old men played cards in the shade; and where Wang, the Artful Dodger of the newspaper-sellers, lurks – the tough boy who protects one from the more rapacious beggars (there are a good many of *them*).

I was pleased to find so many French restaurants open again. And there was one bar, perhaps the best bar in Asia, under the theatre, with a dark atmosphere and good paintings on the walls, and two barmen – Vietnamese, of course – who have become my friends: Billy and Nam. They are both honest young men, too young to remember the war, like many Vietnamese (but perhaps that's no bad thing).

The bar itself, which is called the Q-Bar, is owned and run by David Jacobsen, an American, and his Vietnamese wife. It does very well and is one of the few bars tolerated by the authorities, who are still suspicious of foreigner-owned places of entertainment. I have never seen anything the slightest bit subversive going on there, so the authorities could relax their suspicions; there is nothing to worry about. The Q-Bar is extremely popular with the expatriate community, so I don't know what would happen if Jacobsen did ever have to close down. I told him his bar and one in Hanoi called Gustave's are the best in Southeast Asia. That pleased him no end.

Although the centre of Saigon has changed greatly in many ways as a result of peace and relative plenty, with skyscraper hotels and department stores going up all over the place, the traffic does not seem to have been much affected at all. True, there do seem to be more cars about – taxis mostly – but the majority of vehicles are cyclos (as of old), motorbikes and bicycles. More and more motorbikes are in evidence, which points, I suppose, to the zeal of the Japanese salesmen and their success in selling as well as the population's growing ability to afford the prices. Saigon is a long way from being like Bangkok or Singapore, although foreigners knowingly predict that the worst will occur in a few years' time. There is no visible sign of pollution in Saigon up to now, at any rate.

It is noticeable that the further north you go in Vietnam the fewer cars there are – except for Danang. Nha Trang seems to have very few; Hué, fewer still; and even Hanoi doesn't have nearly so many as Saigon. The main hazard in Hanoi, from the driving point of view, is the appalling danger encountered at major street-crossings: no traffic lights and few policemen add up to a hazardous state of affairs.

Again, in Saigon I felt a great elation because the sound of bombs had stopped, no flares trickled down the night sky; nobody was being killed; even the flood of refugees had come to an end.

I remember leaning from the balustrade of my room in the Majestic (I had rented a room there for two nights in order simply to view the riverside from that priceless vantage point). I looked down on the towering lights of the ocean-going ships in the harbour and the neon of the numerous signs advertising Japanese and American imported goods – Honda, Sony, Coca-Cola, Hewlett Packard. I thought of all those years of war that had gone by. The Vietnamese below me seemed to typify the new Vietnamese as well as the young, carefree Vietnamese I seemed to have left behind me thirty years ago. Today, I thought, the average Vietnamese doesn't want to so much as *think* of the war: he wants a Honda and a fistful of dollars.

I turned away from the window; I felt tired. I was meeting Tam the next day. She was going to take me for a trip up the river that I knew so well by sight but on which I had never been because, during the war, the Viet Cong had been positioned along the far bank.

The Cao Dai Temple at Tay Ninh. The 'ever-open eye of God' can be seen at the top of the picture.

Epilogue

This book is a collection of bits and pieces; a mishmash of the odds and ends of recollections based on old photographs I took when I was young.

I have said in another book that travel for me was never a matter of chance. I ran away to it deliberately, as boys once ran away to sea. I felt that there must be more to do in this world than join the ranks of sombrely suited people sitting behind desks. Sitting at desks was a good way to make money; but money in my view wasn't everything.

What was equally important, or much *more* important, was seeing the world. I have said early in this book that I saw the world as an apple I wanted to devour. This is perfectly true. There is a passage from Joseph Conrad's *Youth*, describing his arrival at Muntok, which is one of the most stimulating invocations to adventure I have ever read:

And this is how I see the East. I see it always from a small boat ... I have the feel of the oar in my hand ... And I see a bay, a wide bay, smooth as glass and polished like ice, shimmering in the dark. A red light burns far off upon the gloom of the land, and the night is soft and warm. We drag at the oars with aching arms, and suddenly a puff of wind comes out of the still night – the first sigh of the East on my face. That I can never forget.

And this is how I myself see the East. I see it as Conrad did; and felt the first sigh of the East on my face, as he did. Like him, I can never forget that. Nor do I want to. Ever.

So this is a tidying-up. I may write other books: I hope so. But for now, this is the summing-up of a life of travel and adventure, the life I promised myself all those years ago.

Forgive the indifferent quality of some of the photographs. I was never a professional photographer; a *paparazzo*, as they say now. I was always a writer and doer. A traveller, in short. As I still am.